The Transforming Power of Lectio Divina

The transforming power *of* LECTIO DIVINA

How to pray with Scripture

Maria Tasto

Second Printing 2015
Twenty-Third Publications
1 Montauk Avenue
Suite 200
New London, CT 06320
(860) 437-3012
(800) 321-0411
www.23rdpublications.com

ISBN: 978-1-58595-922-8
Library of Congress Catalog Card Number: 2013945645
Printed in the U.S.A.

TABLE OF CONTENTS

PREFACE

MANY BOOKS HAVE been written on the method of *lectio divina* as a prayer practice. It is an ancient and yet simple way of praying that is not difficult to make one's own. What is often forgotten is that *lectio divina* is a way to nourish our relationship with God that can have a transformative effect on the faithful practitioner.

Finding time each day to ponder the meaning of the Scriptures, to listen attentively, and to allow the Word of God to speak leads us to discover the deeper meaning of Scripture and opens us to an intimacy with God that knows no words. It slowly changes how we think and how we respond to life's challenges. It puts us in touch with the very ground of our being, where we are one with God's Spirit within us. This transforming power of *lectio divina* frees us from our falsity and slowly draws us into our truth in the light of God's Word. We are shaped into the *word of God* we were created to be; we become not only made in God's image but like God: "I no longer live but Christ lives in me" (Galatians 2:20).

As I retrace my journey of the past few years, I am reminded of the time I was a member of the Resource Faculty of Contemplative Outreach, an international organization founded by Father Thomas Keating, OCSO, whose mission is to teach the practice of centering prayer. As a faculty we often shared ways to support practitioners of centering prayer. In one such discussion the comment was made that a faithful practice of centering prayer inevitably leads to another practice: the prayerful reading of Scripture, or *lectio divina*. This awareness led to the suggestion that as a faculty we create an introductory workshop on *lectio divina*. A committee was formed, which was co-chaired by Father Carl Arico and myself, and we began a process of articulating the ancient practice of *lectio divina* in a way that was easily accessible to the average person. This took the form of presentations clarifying different approaches to *lectio divina* (namely, the monastic and scholastic methods), followed by an opportunity to experience this prayer form. The workshop concluded with a presentation on "Becoming a word of God," which is the inevitable fruit of this practice. I am particularly grateful to the members of this committee for their contributions in the formulation of this workshop.

A second workshop and immersion retreat was eventually created that focused on the monastic form of *lectio divina* and the patristic designation of the four senses of Scripture. As a *lectio divina* service team, we developed the presentations and fine-tuned the interplay between centering prayer and *lectio divina*. I am grateful to Mike Potter (chair), Leslee Anne Terpay, and George Welch for their shared wisdom and the investment of time and energy they brought to this creative endeavor. We also were supported by helpful suggestions from other members of the *lectio divina* service team, namely, Carl Arico, Kathryn Ann Kobelinski, SSND, and Robert Gordon.

It is the culmination of the material contained in these workshops that has been gathered for this book, with a particular emphasis on the transforming power of *lectio divina* via stories that witness this truth. Hopefully, this will provide a simple guide for those who wish to practice *lectio divina* and to grow in understanding the power of the Word of God.

At the end of each chapter on each step or moment of *lectio divina*, there is a simple description of how to approach this aspect of the prayer. Choose one of the books of Scripture, preferably a book of the New Testament, and slowly begin to read it in a *lectio* manner. Use either the scholastic or monastic method, as fits your situation. The scholastic method is the best for learning this way of praying and easily gives way to the monastic method as an ongoing approach to *lectio*.

The end result of our preparation of *lectio divina* workshops continues to be shared in many of the chapters of Contemplative Outreach as well as in other groups in the form of short presentations, workshops, and retreats. All this has deepened the practice of *lectio divina* in the lives of many of the participants. As Pope Benedict XVI remarked:

> *The diligent reading of Sacred Scripture accompanied by prayer brings about that intimate dialogue in which the person reading hears God who is speaking,*

*and in praying, responds to him with trusting openness
(cf. Dei Verbum, n. 25).[1]*

This way of praying, Benedict XVI said, "will bring to the church a new spiritual springtime."[2]

Jean Leclercq describes this springtime in an article on *lectio divina*:

> *Our primary purpose in reading is to acquire the mind of Christ…[3] We are drawn to read Scripture, to find him. We are drawn to read Scripture because he himself did, and because he found himself in Scripture. We are drawn to read Scripture in him and with his grace. Jesus applied to himself the words of Moses, the prophets and the psalms (Lk 24:44). So then must we understand these Old Testament prophets, the gospels and indeed the entire New Testament, if we are truly to understand Jesus' life, his mission and his teaching, and thus come to intimate knowledge in the heart of Jesus.[4]*

Intimate knowledge of the heart of Jesus not only brings this *new springtime*, but it brings into being a new creation. Sister Irene Nowell emphasizes this creative process in an article she wrote on the Word *of* God: "To welcome the word and let it take root in our lives is not only to be created once but to be recreated over and over. Through the word we continue to become a new creation."[5]

This book lends itself to being read in a *lectio* manner. Take a few moments before each reading to become centered and to prepare to listen with the ear of your heart.[6] Make a conscious effort to be aware of God's presence within you and your desire to deepen your relationship with God through the daily practice of *lectio divina*. Then, in unity with others on this journey, pray in a spirit of togetherness:

> Spirit of God, your loving kindness powerfully, yet gently, guides all the moments of our day if we are receptive to your presence. Go before us in our pilgrimage of life, anticipating our needs and teaching us wisdom when we fall. Help us to hear the hidden message in your Word of Scripture so we may respond to your call with integrity, becoming the "word" you created us to be. We ask this through Jesus your Son. Amen.

After each chapter on a specific step or moment of *lectio divina*, take time to choose a passage from Scripture and then practice this aspect of the prayer.

CHAPTER ONE

THE WORD OF GOD

*In the beginning was the Word, and the Word was with God,
and the Word was God. He was in the beginning with God.
All things came into being through him, and without him
not one thing came into being. What has come into being in
him was life, and the life was the light of all people. The light
shines in the darkness, and the darkness did not overcome it.*

JOHN 1:1–5

IN THE PROLOGUE of John's gospel we have a beautiful poetic expression of our Christian faith, our core belief in Jesus as the Word of God. Spoken before time began, Jesus is a Word "that so perfectly and completely expresses the awesome beauty and love of God that this Word itself is God."[7]

Filled with hope and promise, the Word is among us from the beginning, providing us with life and light. Because the Word is the principal way to the Father, we are invited in faith to enter into relationship with this Word of God, Jesus. The Word's transformative power slowly changes us interiorly by guiding us on the path to the Father. As Paul reminds us in his letter to the Romans: "The Spirit helps us in our weakness, for we do not know how to pray as we ought; but...the Spirit intercedes for the saints according to the will of God" (Romans 8:26–27).

To be in relationship with the Word of God, we are invited to take up the Scriptures and listen, ponder, reflect, and rest with Jesus' every action, every word, and every moment. Like the disciples, we need to hear Jesus' message, sit at his feet, learn how he responded to the needs of others, and begin to internalize his way of being and doing. Such an approach to the Word of God is traditionally known as *lectio divina*, sacred reading. It is much like a four-step dance with Jesus: reading, reflecting, responding, and resting with him. It is a natural, organic way of deepening our relationship with Jesus, the Word of God, and coming to an experience of intimacy and oneness. It is an experience of being shaped by the Word of God and coming into fullness as the *word* God created us to be.

It is not, however, without its challenges—as is true of any relationship. Often the message Jesus shared was as confusing to his disciples as it is for us. It sometimes turns our world upside down and leaves us grappling with what he is trying to communicate. When the disciples didn't understand, Jesus would speak in parables to help break through their distortions and limited perceptions. He sometimes grew impatient: "Do you still not perceive or understand? Are your hearts hardened? Do you have eyes and fail to see? And do you not remember?" (Mark 8:17–18).

Knowing that the disciples didn't understand can be

encouraging to us. We know only too well their struggle to comprehend. Our fears of the unknown and our hesitancy to expose our vulnerability also block our understanding. As much as we want intimacy, we are very slow in letting another see us as we are. Yet we need to trust that God will show us the way; and then, slowly, like the disciples, we will began to take on a new way of seeing, a new way of hearing, and a new way of being in relationship. It was the disciples' faith in Jesus that gave them the strength to enter into dialogue and be changed in ways they never could have anticipated.

This new way of being is also in store for us. We can have the same hope in God's promise that God will bring us into fullness of being if we continue to listen to the Word of God. If we are faithful to the practice of *lectio divina* we will experience the fruits of listening, reflecting, responding, and resting with the Word of God. To pray in this way shapes us into being fully the persons we are meant to be. It slowly prepares us to approach all of life in a *lectio* manner. As we begin to read, reflect, respond, and rest with the Scriptures in patient receptivity, the deeper meaning of God's Word will show itself to us, and we will grow in openness to God's presence and action in our lives.

THE HISTORICAL DEVELOPMENT OF *LECTIO DIVINA*

Lectio divina is a method of prayer that finds its roots in the Hebrew approach to the Scriptures called *Haggadah*, which was practiced by the Jewish people in the days of Jesus—they freely interpreted the sacred text in an effort to uncover its deeper meaning. In the early centuries of the Christian era, the Desert Mothers and Fathers understood the gift of this way of praying. They reflected on the Word of God, taking it within and slowly integrating its message. Their relationship with Jesus was fed and deepened by this reflective time and bore fruit as they responded in love. They often referred to this process as an experience of eating food, following the insight of Jeremiah: "Your words were found, and I ate them, and your words became to me a joy and the delight of my heart" (Jeremiah 15:16).

They sank their teeth into Scripture as if it was fresh-baked bread, and they let it nourish them so that they might act upon it in their daily lives. The great Cistercian abbot St. Bernard of Clairvaux writes:

> *Store up the Word of God as you would food. The Word of God is living bread, the food of the soul. Bread kept in a cupboard can be stolen, eaten by rats, go stale, but once it is eaten none of these misfortunes are to be feared. Store up the Word of God like that, because blessed are those that keep it. Let it sink into your inmost heart and pass into your affection and way of life. Eat plentifully of it and your soul will rejoice. Never forget to eat this bread, lest your heart wither, but feed and strengthen it with so rich and fruitful a food. If you hold on to the Word, the Word will protect you. The Son of God will come to you and his Father also.[8]*

This was a way to read the Scriptures that would result in a whole new way of living one's life. Father Raymond

Studzinski, in his book *Reading to Live*, draws on Paul Griffiths' recent study *Religious Reading: The Place of Reading in the Practice of Religion*. Studzinski summarizes Griffiths this way: "To read religiously is to read as a lover, wanting to savor the experience. The religious reader approaches what is to be read with the sense that it is a gold mine of riches that can never be exhausted."[9]

To read in this manner is to open oneself to a transformative experience. Reflection on the Word imprints the Word on one's heart and slowly changes the way one perceives reality and responds to daily life.[10]

This ancient approach to reading the Scriptures was kept alive by the spread of monasticism and the Desert Fathers and Mothers of early Christianity. In their listening to Scripture they envisioned a very free-flowing movement.

> *The early monks read scripture aloud. So they were actually listening to it. They would then choose a phrase (or a sentence at the most) that impressed them. They would sit with that sentence or phrase without thinking of stages or following some predetermined schema, but just listening, repeating slowly the same short text over and over again. This receptive disposition enabled the Holy Spirit to expand their capacity to listen. As they listened, they might perceive a new depth to the text or an expanding meaning. A particular insight might also be singularly appropriate for them in their particular life situation or for the events of the coming day. According to scripture, the Spirit speaks to us every day.[11]*

Listening in this way initiated a deepening level of faith and understanding of the Word of God. These levels of faith were called the four senses of Scripture[12] by monks in the Middle Ages. The four senses of Scripture, or the four levels of faith, are reflected in the different moments of *lectio divina*. The first moment, *lectio*, corresponds to the literal sense of Scripture, *meditatio* to the allegorical sense, *oratio* to the moral sense, and *contemplatio* to the unitive sense. We will consider each of these senses of Scripture as we focus on each moment of *lectio divina*.

The monks' approach was called monastic *lectio divina*. It was a way of being in relationship with the Word of God that moved as if along the circumference of a circle,[13] from the literal to the spiritual level of meaning, challenging and changing the reader. Ultimately, this leads to a contemplative experience of Jesus Christ, a spiritual transformation that graces us with a love for all God's creation.[14]

A more structured approach was introduced during the Middle Ages by a Carthusian monk known as Guigo. In his work *The Ladder of the Monks* he presented the prayer as a ladder with discrete rungs. He sees the ladder as the symbol of the ongoing spiritual exercise that should be all-pervasive in the life of the Christian.[15]

In order to identify the different moments of this prayer, he divides divine reading into separate steps: *lectio*, *meditatio*, *oratio*, and *contemplatio*. We know these today in English as reading, reflecting, responding (prayer), and resting (*contemplatio*n). Guigo describes these steps as different rungs of a ladder leading to God. His approach is more structured and has more of an intellectual propensity.

Because of the influence of his times we call his form of praying the Scriptures "scholastic" *lectio divina*. This form of *lectio divina* lends itself to teaching.

> *Lectio divina, as summarized by Guigo II, is in the first instance a discipline. Its orderly sequence ensures thorough accounting for the text, even its tiniest details, and instills the attitude of intellectual humility, proof against arrogance and superficiality. The methodical pedagogy enables, however, its own self-transcendence; at key moments the sequence is seen to resolve into simultaneity, as its discrete constituents become present dimensions of the experiential moment in a flask of spiritual inspiration or an enthusiastic élan.[16]*

Although the scholastic method enables its own self-transcendence, Guigo's separation of the different moments of *lectio divina* into a number of steps could also lead to a somewhat distorted understanding of the prayer. His historical milieu, beset with heresies and schisms, was marked by suspicion and fear. In its reaction to all these challenges, the church discouraged the practice of contemplative prayer. Mystics were suspect, and only a few were considered worthy of authentic union with God. The gift of *contemplatio*n was not considered available to the ordinary Christian. In response to these concerns the scholastic form of *lectio divina* became a way of listening (*lectio*), reflecting (*meditatio*), and responding (*oratio*) to the Word of God. The final moment of the prayer, resting (*contemplatio*), was lost, and with it went a sense that we are all called to be contemplatives and live in oneness with God. *Lectio* came to mean an intellectual pursuit of a particular text rather than a path to *contemplatio*n.[17] With some exceptions, such as Gertrude of Helfta and other monastic men and women, the practice of scholastic *lectio divina* failed to lead the faithful in the pews to the deeper spiritual meaning of Scripture and its transformative power.

Thankfully, the Second Vatican Council initiated a return to the sources. This opened the door for us to reclaim the ancient practice of *lectio divina* in its full context and to once again be open to the deeper meaning of Scripture and its potential impact on our lives. We can now once again acknowledge our common call to union with God and be open to the gift of *contemplatio*n and its transformative power.

Although the scholastic form of *lectio divina* is appropriate for teaching the practice, it is important to encourage practitioners to eventually move to the more free-flowing movement of the monastic *lectio divina*. This is a progression that takes place as we begin to enter more fully into relationship with God's Word and find ourselves relying on the Word of God as the source that guides us and gives us life.

MANNER OF READING

If we are to read the Scriptures in a way that changes and transforms us, we need to know how to read in a particular manner. In his book *Shaped by the Word*, Robert Mulholland gives an extensive description of two kinds of reading, namely, informational and formational reading. He describes informational reading as a gathering of data and a seeking to cover as much material as possible as quickly as possible. This type of reading is meant to capture the essence of what is being said. We were taught to read this way in school, and so we tend to approach the Bible in the manner of informational reading. This is helpful if we wish to become acquainted with the content of each book of the Scriptures,[18] or to become knowledgeable of the context in which a gospel is written. This type of informational reading or Bible study is intended to master the text,[19] rather than letting the text master us. At times it is an excellent precursor of the formational reading of the Scriptures. If, however, we wish to pray the Scriptures, we need to engage in formational reading.

The formational reading of *lectio divina* is about quality, not quantity. It involves spending time with a word or phrase that catches our attention. It is *listening* "with the ear of our heart" as Saint Benedict encourages us to do at the beginning of his Rule.[20] When we listen from this stance, we are attentive to what stirs within us, to what touches us. It is a way of listening that engages both the mind and the heart. We might find ourselves asking: what is this passage saying to me? What would I learn if I spent a whole year with this book of the Bible?

Sometimes we may find that a particular text does not speak to us. At such times it may be helpful to read the text again, noting any consonance or dissonance we feel in relationship to it. The key to uncovering the multiple meanings of the text is to linger with the text, reading it over and over, and waiting in patience until we are drawn to—or find ourselves resisting—one of its words or phrases. In this kind of reading we let ourselves be vulnerable to the text; we are willing to be touched, to be changed, to be formed by it. We will hear God's message for us as the multiple layers of meaning unfold.

This formational reading approaches the text as the subject of our relationship with God. We are the object shaped by the text. We are the ones who are called to change. For example, consider the story of the prodigal son. In this parable, the father represents the law. It is his responsibility to enforce the law within his family. According to that law, the father should reject his younger son. That would have been the expected outcome for the Jewish community. Instead, the father rejects the rigidity of the law, embraces his son, welcomes him home, and celebrates with him and the whole household. This angers the older son, who has faithfully abided by the law. But, even with just cause, the father does not chastise this older son for his outburst of anger. Instead, the father responds to his elder son in love: "you are always with me, and all that is mine is yours"(Luke 15:31).

The overriding message of this story is that God the Father does not reject anyone and that we are generously given everything we need. We have no claim on God's love. It is pure gift—so the divine inheritance doesn't belong to us or anyone else.[21] Such a message challenges our way of thinking, our value system. It doesn't fit our insistence on doing the right thing or an either/or way of thinking. The text takes us outside our comfort zone. If we are willing to engage with the text—asking our questions, examining our judgments, letting a new way of responding find a place within us—then we will be changed by the text. This kind of formational reading requires a humble, detached, receptive, and loving approach to the text. We have to step outside of our problem-solving mentality and come prepared to dip into the mystery of God given to us through Jesus, the inspired Word of God.

We find this same challenge in the science of quantum physics. In the documentary *What the Bleep Do We Know?* our sense of reality is called into question as the laws of physics demonstrate that what we believe to be a solid block of wood is actually a cluster of molecules in relationship. As the film begins, a commentator says: "We always want to be in the know. The challenge is to be in the mystery."[22]

This is our challenge as we enter into the prayer of *lectio divina*. We are invited to be open to the mystery of God, to be willing to be surprised, and to hear something we have never heard before or even envisioned. Then, as we let ourselves be shaped by the Word of God, we will be slowly transformed into a person fully alive, filled with the glory of God.

CHAPTER TWO

THE VESTIBULE

For God alone my soul waits in silence; from God comes my salvation. God alone is my rock and my salvation, my fortress; I shall never be shaken.

PSALM 62:1–2

ENTERING INTO A relationship with the Word of God is a summons to come prepared to listen and to be transformed. This implies an openness and receptivity to the Word of God that enables us to take it in and let it take root and grow within us. As in any relationship, our attitudes toward the other person have a great influence on how we will grow in relationship or grow apart. As God reaches out to us in unconditional love, calling us "to share…in the oneness of the Father and the Son,"[23] we need to ask for the grace to come defenseless to the relationship, ready to be influenced. Such a vulnerability calls for a deep sense of trust, a freedom to listen with reverence and humility, as well as openheartedness and a commitment of fidelity that frees us to surrender ourselves into the loving embrace of God. These attitudes are essential prerequisites if we hope to grow in our relationship with God's Word. It behooves us, then, to reflect on them and acknowledge both our strengths and limitations in their regard.

PREPARATORY ATTITUDES FOR *LECTIO DIVINA*

Trust

And now, thus says Yahweh, he who created you, Jacob, who formed you, Israel: Do not be afraid, for I have redeemed you; I have called you by your name, you are mine.

ISAIAH 43:1

A freedom to trust is probably one of the greatest challenges in any relationship. Trust usually develops as we move through a continuum of knowing, desiring, and surrendering our desires and fears—and ultimately our very selves—to the Beloved. Trust grows in prayer as we faithfully pick up the Scriptures, listen to the meaning of the text, let it speak to our lives, and respond with a deepening desire to simply be with God and to take on the mind and heart of Jesus Christ. In time we begin to trust that God is present and speaks to us through the inspired Word of God working profoundly within our hearts and changing us at a deep level. We are brought to a deepening experience of God's unconditional love, and we find that we are able to trust this love as we are led into the unknown.

As we grow in trust of God's unconditional love, our fears

and insecurities drop away. We are able to let go of our ego defenses and receive God's love so that we in turn can share with others. We experience such trust in the words of a nine-year-old girl who had just been told she had cancer. She said to her parents: "I feel like God is laying down a golden brick path in front of us. We're behind God, so we can't see where it is going, but it's OK because we can see who is laying it."[24]

Reverence and Humility

Then you will call upon me and come and pray to me, and I will listen to you. You will seek me and find me when you seek me with all your heart. I will be found by you, declares the Lord.

JEREMIAH 29:12–14

Such trust prepares us to listen with reverence, with a sense of awe before the mystery of God. This sense of awe before God leads us to become silent, and it opens us to let God's Word fall on the open space within us. We are able to receive the Word as a revelatory text from God and hear God's Word to us. When we bring a reverence to our prayerful reading of the text, we come as disciples being instructed by God: "Morning by morning he makes my ear alert to listen like a disciple. Lord Yahweh has opened my ear and I have not resisted, I have not turned away" (Isaiah 50:4b–5).

As disciples sitting at the feet of the master, we are attentive to every word, every gesture. We listen, we hear, and we begin to understand the life of Jesus and his relationship with the Father, Abba, and we begin to see it as a kind of blueprint—a mentoring experience of how we can be in relationship with God, with ourselves, with one another, and with all of creation.

Such surrender not only flows from a sense of awe in the Beloved, but also from a humble, childlike spirit that is willing to listen. When we have a humble attitude we know that we are in need of God's saving grace in the face of our unworthiness and our distorted desire to earn God's love. It is the humble spirit who is eventually graced with a deepening knowledge that God loves us not because of our worthiness but because God is love and reaches out to us in love. Then we can accept God's love not for our accomplishments but simply because we are. As one woman expressed so simply: "I have spent my life trying to get God to love me and now I am finding out that God can't help but love me."[25]

Such humility is being in touch with the truth, accepting reality as it is—seeing our limitations and our giftedness, as well as God's unconditional love. The attitudes of reverence and humility free us to relate to God and discover who God is and who we are. We come to know that, as Mother Teresa often expressed: "We are but pencils in the hand of God."

Openheartedness

O Lord, open thou my lips, and my mouth shall show forth thy praise. The sacrifice acceptable to God is a broken spirit; a broken and contrite heart, O God, you will not despise.

PSALM 51:15, 17

As we grow in trust, reverence, and humility, an attitude of openheartedness grows within us, and we are able to enter more fully into the unfolding mystery of God. This attitude manifests itself in our being able to more easily let go of the running train of thoughts and related distortions and illusions that fill our minds, along with any preconceived ideas we have about the text. It frees us to listen to the unexpected and to embrace the new and different in the text, reading it *as if for the first time.* Such an attitude of openheartedness prepares us to surrender to the unknown, letting God's Word shape and form us into God's likeness. The Curé of Ars, a revered spiritual director, encouraged this attitude in his directees. He is quoted as saying: "Open your heart so that the Word of God may enter it, take root in it, and bear fruit for eternal life."[26]

Faithfulness

The steadfast love of the Lord never ceases, his mercies never come to an end; they are new every morning; great is your faithfulness.

LAMENTATIONS 3:22–23

As in any healthy relationship, intimacy develops and the relationship deepens as we invest ourselves and are faithful to the practice day in and day out. It takes patience, dedication, and persistence. Spasmodic bursts of devotion do not work. We might compare our faithfulness to boiling water on the stove. A slow, steady application of heat will bring water to a boil more quickly than short, inconsistent bursts of heat. Each application of heat builds with a cumulative effect on that which preceded it, until the water reaches the boiling point and is transformed. It is such faithfulness that is essential if our relationship with God is to become the transforming reality in our lives.

Being faithful is difficult because we are pulled in many different directions in our daily activities. We also find that, as we are faithful, our prayer often becomes dry and arid. We may experience a time of darkness when our path is obscure.

At such times our natural facilities of satisfaction and fervor seem to close down. Our experience of God's presence becomes one of absence and silence. Discursive *meditation* seems meaningless, and we find ourselves attracted to solitary prayer.

An experience of darkness such as this is often God's way of freeing us of the chains that bind us. God purifies our illusions and false beliefs as we are led through what is experienced as a dark experience of God's love. Like Job we need to wait patiently, persevere with fortitude, and be confident in God's faithfulness. During such times when God seems distant and absent, only faith sustains us as we continue to surrender ourselves to God's healing grace.

ADDITIONAL PREPARATIONS

Beginning a time of *lectio divina* with a prayer to the Holy Spirit is a way of asking for the attitudes we need as we reflect on the Scriptures. It is also praying for the grace to be attentive to the Word we are reading and to what it stirs within us. It is helpful to quiet our body and mind in order to bring our whole person into a single focus, open to the Word of God. [27]

Another very significant preparation is to engage in some Bible study regarding the passage with which we are praying. This can include gathering of background information on the culture of the time, identifying the various sources of a particular book of the Bible and its literary genre, and exploring the meaning of a Hebrew or Greek word. We can also do some cross-referencing to compare similar passages as well as search out particular theological themes that impact the meaning of the passage. Although all these avenues of study are helpful, we need to limit our study so that we can give quality time to our prayerful reading of the Scripture passage we have chosen. For the sake of preserving our *lectio* time, *The HarperCollins Study Bible* is a very efficient tool to help us understand the context and meaning of a particular passage. This resource, along with the *Dictionary of Biblical Theology*, can give us a sense of the intent of the gospel writer.

Finally, in order to prepare ourselves to listen, we must begin by entering into the silence. As the passage in the First Book of Kings directs us:

> *Go out and stand on the mountain before the Lord; for the Lord is about to pass by. Now there was a great wind, so strong that it was splitting mountains and breaking rocks in pieces before the Lord, but the Lord was not in the wind; and after the wind an earthquake, but the Lord was not in the earthquake; and after the earthquake a fire, but the Lord was not in the fire; and after the fire a sound of sheer silence. When Elijah heard it, he wrapped his face in his mantle and went out and stood at the entrance of the cave. (1 Kings 19:11–13)*

Silence prepares our hearts to receive God's mystery. "We enter the land of silence by the silence of surrender."[28] Only in the silence can we hear God speak.

Having prepared ourselves by becoming quiet within,

and praying to the Holy Spirit for a trusting, open, and humble spirit, we pick up the Scriptures and choose a passage. We may use the liturgical readings for the day or choose a book of the Bible and slowly read a few verses. We read the passage of Scripture we have chosen with the intent of listening to the words as though for the first time. Our intent is to hear the message, the essence of what is being communicated. We read until we feel the call of the Spirit. Keating describes this ancient way of praying: "doing *lectio divina* does not mean reading a lot. It means reading the text until you feel the call of the Spirit to reflect on a particular passage that you have read or heard."[29]

CHAPTER THREE

LECTIO: LISTENING WITH THE EAR OF OUR HEARTS

Incline your ear and come to me. Listen so that you may live.
For as the rain and the snow come down from heaven, and do
not return there until they have watered the earth, making it
bring forth and sprout, giving seed to the sower and bread to the
eater, so shall my word be that goes out from my mouth; it shall
not return to me empty, but it shall accomplish that which I
purpose, and succeed in the thing for which I sent it.

ISAIAH 55:3, 10–11

THIS FIRST STEP or moment in *lectio divina* is called *lectio*, or reading. It is listening to the literal sense of the word, that is, the meaning intended by the author and the example of Jesus. Our natural tendency in conversation is to stay with our own thoughts and to make presumptions about what is being said. We miss what the other person is really saying and often respond in a way that confirms our perspectives and judgments. Entering into a dialogue relationship with

Scripture has the same pitfalls. We can easily fall into the trap of concluding our prayer with an affirmation of what we thought we heard in Scripture and then continuing to live out of our blindness. In order to avoid this temptation, we need to set aside our presumptions of what God is saying and listen *as though for the first time*. We need to let God take the lead in the conversation as we open ourselves to the unexpected, the disconcerting, and the surprising.

Henri Matisse, a French artist, learned well the importance of approaching something familiar with a fresh awareness. As a young man, Henri was anticipating attending law school after he received his university degree. The summer after his graduation, he found himself at his parents' home recuperating from an unexpected surgery. He spent many hours sitting on his parents' patio, contemplating the beautiful flowers that were planted in his mother's garden. For the first time Henri looked intently at the flowers and saw the depth of their bright colors, the varying hues and shades that complemented each other. Deeply affected by the beauty of the flowers, Henri made a decision that changed the direction of his life. He decided that he wanted to become an artist so he might capture the natural beauty of the flowers that had spoken to him as he focused on their uniqueness and their brilliance. He is quoted as saying: "To *look* at something as though for the first time takes great courage."[30]

We can apply this same principle to the reading of Scripture. It takes great courage to listen as though for the first time. Hearing the words of Scripture with an open, receptive mind and heart will stir possibilities within us. We will be drawn into considerations and decisions we had not anticipated, and our lives will be changed forever.

THE LITERAL SENSE

This first level of meaning we listen for in *lectio divina* is what the patristic fathers called the literal sense of Scripture. It is the meaning intended by the author. Of course, a text may have more than one literal sense—as when an author wishes to refer at one and the same time to more than one level of reality. The writers sometimes use poetry, history, parables, and hymns to get their various points across. But however they express themselves, they all have a meaning they intend to communicate. This sense of Scripture is not to be confused with the *literalist* sense to which fundamentalists are attached. One must understand the text according to the literary conventions of the time.[31] This makes hearing the meaning of the author contingent on our understanding of its context. We need to listen in an open and receptive way. Because we have heard much of Scripture, we tend to assume what the author is going to say and get blinded by this familiarity. Our challenge is to hear what the human author is trying to say, the way in which he was trying to say it. It's fitting to review commentaries and check annotations and cross-references as we try to hear the message the author is trying to express—the meaning that God had thought well to manifest through the medium of words.

Sometimes, as we prayerfully read a passage from Scripture, we will find that nothing stirs within us. This experience often heightens a sense of separateness from God that we are feeling. We wonder why God is not speaking to us. A Jewish boy was puzzling about such a situation. He approached his rabbi and asked: "Rabbi, why does God no longer speak to his people? He spoke so beautifully to Abraham. He spoke with such power to Moses. He spoke so clearly to Jeremiah and the prophets. Rabbi, why does God no longer speak to his people?" The Rabbi silently shook his head. Tears welled up in his eyes. "My son," he replied, "it is not that God no longer speaks to his people. It is that no one these days can stoop down low enough to listen. No one…can stoop down low enough to listen."[32]

Listening to the Word of God challenges us to stoop down lower than we have ever stooped before. In other words, we need to step out of our world and into the world of Jesus. We need to come defenseless, ready to be influenced. We need to be willing to be vulnerable, open to learn, to change, and to be transformed. This may entail a level of listening that we have never engaged in before.

This is true receptivity to the Word—to take it in and let it speak to us. This is the challenge of *lectio divina*. It is about entering into relationship with the Word. A research scientist who worked with different breeds of corn was once asked why she was so good at what she did. She replied: "It is because I lean into the kernel."

When we lean into something, we are in relationship to it. It's not an object to be analyzed and conceptualized. As we enter into a prayerful listening to the Word of God, *lectio*, we need to lean into the Scriptures by reading the passage over slowly, allowing the Word to convey the meaning intended by the author. What we hear may be more than words can convey. Sometimes it is helpful to read the text aloud, allowing the words to penetrate every level of our being. As a word or phrase in the text resonates with us, we sit with it, listening with the ear of the heart,[33] savoring it, allowing it to repeat itself over and over in our consciousness, and welcoming it in faith. We don't think about the text but just let it awaken within us—and we listen to it in a spirit of silence and awe.

There is a subtle difference between listening and reflecting. So often we do not listen as deeply as we could. We tend to rush right into reflective thoughts and miss the real point of the conversation. The time spent in listening to the Word, *lectio*, is hanging out with the reading—letting it go to a deeper level within us. We savor it and try to stay with the word or phrase that catches our attention, hearing WHAT is being said. It is not necessary to identify a precise meaning of the text. Simply "being with" the Word in a disposition of love and trust is sufficient. This process is analogous to coming to meet the other with the intention of sharing time together alone and anticipating an exchange that will deepen our growing relationship.[34]

A SCHOLASTIC METHOD OF *LECTIO DIVINA*

PRELIMINARY COMMENTS

The scholastic method of lectio divina is a structured approach to this prayer form. There are four distinct steps, each one corresponding to a different aspect of the prayer. This method of lectio divina is helpful when teaching and when praying in a group setting.

LECTIO: LISTENING TO THE WORD OF GOD OR READING GOD'S WORD

- Become quiet and consciously aware of God's presence. Pray for the gifts to listen with trust, humility, reverence, openness, and faith. Choose a passage from Scripture. Listen to the Word of God as if for the first time; be aware of any word or phrase that catches your attention—a word or phrase.

- Begin to repeat that phrase, sentence, or one word over and over, allowing it to settle deeply in your heart. If any insights arise, do not expand these insights right now. This can be done at a later time. Simply return to the slow repetition of the phrase, sentence, or one word, savoring it in your heart.

- If so moved, share the word or phrase that caught your attention in the reading (applies to group setting).

- Allow a few moments of silence so that what was heard may sink deeper within.

A MONASTIC METHOD OF *LECTIO DIVINA*

PRELIMINARY COMMENTS

The monastic way is unstructured—in a sense, methodless. One reads or listens to the Word of God in a particular passage chosen for the occasion, and then the only process is to follow the attraction of the Spirit. As one is faithful to the practice of lectio divina, one naturally moves from the more structured scholastic approach to the free-flowing monastic form of lectio divina.

THE MOMENT OF *LECTIO*

- Read the Scripture passage for the first time (it helps to read it aloud softly). What phrase, sentence, or even one word stands out to you? Begin to repeat that phrase, sentence, or one word over and over, allowing it to settle deeply in your heart. If any insights arise, do not expand them right now. This can be done at a later time. Simply return to the slow repetition of the phrase, sentence, or one word, savoring it in your heart.
- Relish these words; let them resound in your heart. Read the passage as often as you wish, learning these words by heart as you continue to repeat them in your mind.
- Let an attitude of quiet receptiveness—an openness to a deeper hearing of the Word of God—permeate your prayer time.

CHAPTER FOUR

MEDITATIO: REFLECTING WITH TRUST AND OPENNESS

I will bless God at all times;
words of praise are ever in my mouth.
I glory in the Most High;
let the humble hear and rejoice.

O magnify the Holy One with me;
together let us praise God's name.
When I called for help God answered
and freed me of all my fears.

Look to God and be radiant with joy;
your faces will not be ashamed.
The afflicted call out in distress
and are heard by God and rescued.

An angel keeps guard and will protect
all those who fear the Most High.
Taste and see the goodness of God.

Be happy! Make the Holy One your refuge!

Remain faithful; revere the Most High.
Those who fear God will lack nothing.
The strong may know want and go hungry,
but those who seek God lack no blessing.

PSALM 34:1–10

PSALM 34 IS a song of praise to God, who "frees us of all our fears and rescues us from our distress." This deliverance is promised "for those who fear the Most High." As we reflect on this psalm, we may find ourselves being drawn closer to a God who offers us protection—and yet pulling away from a God we are to fear. Such quandaries are to be expected when we ponder the meaning of Scripture. Often the perspective of Scripture turns our world upside down and challenges us in ways we did not anticipate. The key in this song of praise is to understand the range of meaning of "fear" in biblical literature. "Fear of the Lord" can and often does have the meaning of reverencing and honoring God. It is an experience of quiet awe in the face of a love that knows no bounds. It can also be an all-encompassing term for worship and obedience. In verse seven we find that "An angel keeps guard and will protect all those who fear the Most High." Here fearing God evokes God's protection.[35] "Fear of the Lord" is an attitude and stance of the holy. This specific meaning of "fear" in Psalm 34 helps us grasp the literal sense of the psalm—the intention of the author—and frees us to reflect on the meaning the text has for our personal life.

MEDITATION

The term "meditation" is used to describe many ways of praying. It can refer to either a letting go of the inner thoughts that often occupy our mind or a more concentrative approach to a particular Scripture passage or text. Centering prayer is a practice of letting go of one's thoughts with the intent of consenting to God's presence and action in our lives. The more concentrative approach was encouraged by Ignatius of Loyola in his Spiritual Exercises. He used a method of imagining that helps us concentrate on the deeper meaning of the text. In this method, we place ourselves in the Scripture passage, becoming one of the persons in the story. This helps us discover how we are in relationship with Jesus—as we become the leper being healed, the man being lowered through the roof, or the woman at the well asking for the water Jesus offered. This is a type of discursive meditation that "engages thought, imagination, emotion, and desire. This mobilization of faculties deepens our convictions of faith, prompts the conversion of our heart, and strengthens our will to follow Christ."[36]

In *lectio divina* the approach to *meditatio*, meditation, is to ponder the meaning of a passage of Scripture for our life. We begin by asking ourselves:

- What catches my attention?
- What does this passage stir within me? How does it touch my life?

As we ponder our response to such questions, we are often touched in a way that prompts further questions, insights, and new awareness. The story is told of a young disciple who said to his master: "I have gone through all the Scriptures and memorized them. Now what should I do?" The master looked at him kindly and said, "Yes, you have gone through all the Scriptures, but have you let the Scriptures go through you?"

In meditation we let the Scriptures go through us. We are attentive to what stirs within us as we ponder the words. We hold them and wait upon them as they speak to us. We may find ourselves entering into dialogue with the Word, asking our questions, pondering the full meaning of the text as it impacts our life.

This pondering is a central activity of *meditatio*. According to the ancient Greeks, to ponder meant to analyze, to think about something intellectually, and to contemplate God's mysteries. But to ponder something in the biblical sense means to simply hold it, be with it, and let it open of its own accord. We look to Mary as one who knew how to ponder in the face of mystery. At the birth of Jesus, "Mary listened to the shepherds, treasuring and pondering their words in her heart" (Luke 2:19). This pondering continued even to the foot of the cross as she watched her son breathe his last. Again she held the experience within her—just being with the experience and trusting that, in time, understanding would come to her.

The tendency we have, however, is to expect immediate results and to try to bring about desired outcomes as we reflect upon the Scriptures. We are much like a young boy who wanted to give a beautiful rose to his mother as a way to thank her for the birthday party she had hosted for him.

When he went to the rose garden looking for a rose in full bloom, he found only rosebuds. Disappointed he decided to pick a rosebud. He then proceeded to open it one petal at a time. As he pulled the petals down, the rosebud fell apart. In the end he had nothing to give his mother but a sad-looking stem without a flower.

If we pull apart and analyze a particular Scripture passage, we often block the movement of the Spirit within us. We lose the deeper meaning that is conveyed in the words of Scripture. Rather, we need to ponder the text by accepting it as we receive it and by letting it speak to us. We need to wait patiently and be attentive to what stirs within us, listening to hear the message it is conveying on our behalf. Such pondering in this second moment of *lectio divina* is not a passive response. It is a waiting in silence until a question stirs within us or a dialogue begins to shape itself. You may find yourself asking God:

- Why haven't I noticed this before?

- How does this message affect my life?

- What is God trying to say to me?

ALLEGORICAL SENSE

As we begin to interiorize the events of the Scriptures, we slowly begin to realize that the gospel is about us, that our lives are mirrored in its pages. The Scriptures become stories about our own life journey. This is the allegorical sense that is explored in the second moment of *lectio divina*, and it opens for us the deeper meaning of the text. We open ourselves to God's Word and let God's Spirit lead and guide us as the words of Scripture speak to our lives. We bring to the prayer our unique relationship with God and listen intuitively for the deeper meaning of the Scripture message. This is the voice that speaks—in symbol, metaphor, and story.[37] One person may explore the meaning of the text more effectively by means of imagination into a gospel scene, seeing or hearing persons, etc., while another may gain more by savoring the truth or insight inherent in the passage, deeply interiorizing what is being said in the text. Ultimately, only the Holy Spirit can teach us to pray, and all anyone else can do is to dispose oneself to receive that teaching experientially.[38]

The allegorical sense of Scripture draws upon our intuitive level of understanding—thus, words give way to hidden meanings. If we are open and willing to be vulnerable, our identification with our false self—with its habitual expectations, demands, or "shoulds"—is challenged. We are slowly freed to confront the darker side of our personality and enter into a purification process. Our ideas, programs, and plans are also exposed to the light of Scripture, and the wax in our ears is removed. We hear the text addressed to us—the allegorical sense—and our lives are forever changed. We are shaped by the Word and become who God intended us to be.[39]

NOTICING A WORD OR PHRASE

A helpful way to listen to the meaning of a particular passage is to notice what catches our attention. Experiencing a sense of dissonance or consonance with the text is a good indication that we need to stop and listen attentively to what is being said. I remember directing a woman during a thirty-day retreat. She was a very kind, gentle woman who had spent her whole life dedicated to God's Word. I asked her to reflect on a passage from the Old Testament that contained some expression of violence. After reflecting on it, she came back and said: "I've tried to be a peaceful, gentle woman all my life, and I do not like this passage."

I asked her to go back to the passage and spend the entire day with it. She did so, reluctantly. After listening to it for the day, lingering with it in the silence, she was able to identify the source of her resistance. She found that she did not want to own the subtle traces of violence she carried deep within herself. This passage became the most transformative experience of her retreat. She grew both in self-knowledge and in humility; she experienced God's unconditional love, compassion, and forgiveness in a way that shifted her perception of self and others.

THE SKILL OF LISTENING

Our ability to reflect, to ponder the Word of God, is greatly impacted by how well we can listen. Listening is a difficult skill to learn. We usually consider the ability to listen a natural gift if our hearing is not impaired. But although we have two ears and our physical capability to hear is excellent, we may be very poor listeners. In order to listen and hear what another is saying, we need to step out of our world and into theirs. We need to look at the world from their perspective and hear the message they are trying to communicate.

This is our challenge in *lectio divina*, as it is in any relationship. Many years ago I witnessed the healing that is possible when we are able to listen. I went to a workshop in Dubuque, Iowa, given by Fr. Charles Curran, a Jesuit priest and psychologist from Chicago. He said that if we really listen we can be co-redeemers with God in the lives of other people. He said listening to someone does not take a long time. Rather, it involves a surrender of our world and a willingness to step into the world of another. Father Curran asked for a volunteer to come forward to demonstrate the power of true listening. He asked that this person be someone who was struggling with a problem that was causing them a good deal of stress. I remember wondering if anyone would have the courage to come forward and share a personal problem in front of ninety workshop participants.

But without too much hesitation, a young woman volunteered to share her problem. She was young and well-dressed, and appeared to be very secure. But when she took the microphone, she was clutching it so tight we could see the whiteness of her knuckles. She asked us not to laugh as she told Fr. Curran that she struggled with a terrible fear of flying. She explained that she worked for a large book company and was required to travel all over the world. "I get so upset and anxious before I fly," she said, "that I get testy with everyone. I'm ready to jump down everyone's throat."

Father Curran asked her to tell us what happens when she boards a flight.

"Well," she said, "when I get on the flight, first of all, I walk toward my seat, noticing that others are already seated, reading newspapers or magazines. They seem so relaxed, and the more relaxed they seem the more nervous I get! Finally I reach my seat and settle into place. I can't read or concentrate on anything, and my heart is in my throat. My mouth gets dry, and I clutch the sides of my seat as the plane prepares to take off."

As she described the situation, she became more and more agitated. Father Curran, standing off to the side, began to reflect her great fear on his face. He said to her, "You are paralyzed, aren't you?"

She responded, "Yes, I do become paralyzed. Everything inside of me comes to a halt, and I can hardly breathe!"

It was evident by the look of fear on Father Curran's face that he was standing in her world, feeling her paralysis. All of a sudden she began to laugh. "Isn't this ridiculous, to be so frightened?" she said.

As she saw her own fear on Father Curran's face, she was able to see her fear objectively for the first time. This freed her to let go of her fear to some degree. After a moment of silence she thanked Fr. Curran and said: "I don't think I will ever again have as much fear about flying."

When we listen to another in this way—taking on their emotions, fears, and anxieties—they are able to see their feelings on our face. Looking at her situation objectively, this young woman was less fearful. Of course, some of us thought this demonstration of listening had been staged. Several participants approached the young woman and asked her if she had prearranged this with Father Curran. She assured them that she had not. At the end of the workshop she stepped forward and said, "I know some of you think this was staged, but I had never met Father Curran before today. We did not discuss or arrange this beforehand. But now, I don't think I will be as afraid to fly as I was before. I'll write to you and let you know how I'm doing."

After six months we received a letter from her describing all the cities she had flown to in Japan, Europe, and the United States. "I still don't like to fly," she wrote, "but I no longer have the fear I used to have."

If our listening to one another can be healing, imagine the healing power of Scripture in our lives if we truly listen to God's Word. *Lectio divina* is a way of praying that leads us into God's world. If we want to hear God's Word we need to step out of our own world and let our *word*, our spirit, be touched by God's Word, God's Spirit. We do this by listening, *lectio*, to God's Word as though for the first time and then reflecting on the message, *meditatio*, on an intuitive level. As God made his dwelling among us (John 1:14), so we need to make our dwelling in God's Word. This is not easy. It means letting go of our defenses and being open and receptive to God's healing power as the walls we have erected to protect ourselves are slowly dismantled. This bending the ear of our hearts—leaning into God's Word, standing in God's world—is the way we need to listen to the stirrings within us.

BEING WITH THE WORD

If we can step into God's Word, God will reveal to us the truth. Finding God's truth comes not by our analyzing, rationalizing, or intellectualizing the meaning of God's Word, but rather by being open and receptive to what stirs within us, resting in silence with the Word until it speaks to us. This is *lectio divina*—hearing the Word as if for the first time, waiting upon the Word, entering into dialogue, living in the Word, and surrendering to it. Just as Father Curran allowed himself to be drawn into this young woman's story, we need to let ourselves be drawn into the Word of God. If nothing stirs within us, we need to read the passage or verse over and over again and simply be with it. We may find ourselves resting in the quiet. In time it will speak and reveal its meaning for us.

Lectio divina, then, is not an intellectual exercise. We are not thinking about the text; we are being with it. As we repeat the word or phrase that catches our attention, we are, so to speak, being marinated in the Word, being brought to its fuller meaning. This patient soaking in the Word and pondering it is similar to a cow ruminating, chewing its cud. The cow has several stomachs, requiring that it chew over and over again as part of the digestive process. In *lectio divina*, our digestive process involves pondering, reflecting on, and repeating the Word over and over. This is not about production or coming to grand insights. It's simply about being with the Word, letting it speak and penetrate our depths. As a practical example, look at a phrase from Matthew's gospel: "But the Son of Man has nowhere to lay his head" (Mt 8:20). Reflect for a moment on that image—no security, no safety, no place to call home. What would that be like? In order to really listen to and understand this situation, we would have to let go of our many securities and let ourselves experience God as our only security. When we listen to God—hearing the Word and responding to it—God slowly, gently, gives us the grace we need to stand in the truth of his Word.

St. Francis de Sales once compared meditation, *meditatio*, with sitting before a fire in the wintertime. After logs are put on the fire, we sit back and watch it, and we slowly become mesmerized as the flames work their way in between the logs. If we put too many logs on the fire we will kill it. Meditating, pondering the Word, is similar to putting logs on a fire. After reading the Word as though for the first time, we sit back and just rest with the Word, letting it draw us in. We simply let it happen, just as the fire finds its own life. At times we may need to reread the passage, as if we were putting new logs on the fire. We feed our being with the Word just enough to continue to be open and receptive to its meaning for us. If we add too many thoughts, we may kill the new fire that is trying to emerge. Keating describes the heart of *lectio divina* this way:

> *The heart of the prayer is to recognize the presence and action of God and to consent to it. We do not have to go anywhere; God is already with us. Effort refers to the future and to what we do not yet have. Consent refers to the present moment and its content. Faith tells us that we already have God—the divine indwelling. The most intimate relationship with God is to be completely present to God in whatever we are doing. In this sense, prayer is a preparation for life. What we do in silence under ideal circumstances, we begin to do in daily life, remaining in the interior freedom we experienced during contemplative prayer even in the midst of intense activity.*[40]

JOURNALING

During our time of reflecting on a particular passage, we may find it helpful to journal about the passage. Sometimes this can be done in the form of a dialogue with God. When we write a dialogue, we simply record what we want to say to God and then what we believe God would say to us. We allow the dialogue to have its own life, to go in directions we had not anticipated. We ask our questions, make our comments, and express our feelings. We record how God might respond to us—God's comments, questions, and words of guidance. This process of dialoguing was part of the Intensive Journal Method developed by Dr. Ira Progoff in the 1970s. It is one way of moving toward the more intuitive level of understanding as we engage in the moment of *meditatio*. Even though there is no audible voice, we are being called to ponder, listen, and enter into the mystery of God contained in a particular passage of Scripture. In time, new vistas, new ways of perceiving the ordinary, will open before us.

A SCHOLASTIC METHOD OF *LECTIO DIVINA*

PRELIMINARY COMMENTS

The scholastic method of lectio divina *is a structured approach to this way of praying. There are four distinct steps, each one corresponding to a different aspect of the prayer. This method of* lectio divina *is helpful when teaching and when praying in a group setting. This exercise involves both the first and second moments of* lectio divina: lectio *and* meditatio.

LECTIO: LISTENING TO THE WORD OF GOD OR READING GOD'S WORD

- Become quiet and consciously aware of God's presence. Pray for the gifts to listen with trust, humility, reverence, openness, and faith. Choose a passage from Scripture and read it as though for the first time.
- Listen to the Word of God as if for the first time; be aware of any word or phrase that catches your attention—a word or phrase.
- Begin to repeat that phrase, sentence, or one word over and over, allowing it to settle deeply in your heart. If any insights arise, do not expand these insights right now. This can be done at a later time. Simply return to the slow repetition of the phrase, sentence, or one word, savoring it in your heart.
- If so moved, share the word or phrase that caught your attention in the reading (applies to group setting).
- Allow a few moments of silence so that what was heard may sink deeper within.

MEDITATIO: PONDERING ITS MEANING

- Read the chosen passage from Scripture a second time.
- Notice what stirs within as you repeat the word or phrase that catches your attention.
- What is God saying?
- If moved to do so, share what stirs within in response to the word or phrase that caught your attention (applies in group setting).
- Allow a few moments of silence so that what was heard may sink deeper within.

A MONASTIC METHOD OF *LECTIO DIVINA*

PRELIMINARY COMMENTS

The monastic way is unstructured—in a sense, methodless. One reads or listens to the Word of God in a particular passage chosen for the occasion, and then the only process is to follow the attraction of the Spirit.

THE MOMENT OF *LECTIO*

- Read the Scripture passage for the first time (it helps to read it aloud softly). What phrase, sentence, or even one word stands out to you? Begin to repeat that phrase, sentence, or one word over and over, allowing it to settle deeply in your heart. If any insights arise, do not expand these insights right now. This can be done at a later time. Simply return to the slow repetition of the phrase, sentence, or one word, savoring it in your heart.

- Relish these words; let them resound in your heart. Read the passage as often as you wish, learning these words by heart as you continue to repeat them in your mind.

- Let an attitude of quiet receptiveness permeate your prayer time—an openness to a deeper hearing of the Word of God.

THE MOMENT OF *MEDITATIO*

- Let an attitude of quiet receptiveness permeate your prayer time: be open to a deeper hearing of the Word of God.

- Sit with that phrase, sentence, insight, or word, repeating it gently over and over in your heart, not *thinking about it* but just being with it (pondering it in your heart).

CHAPTER FIVE

ORATIO: RESPONDING WITH COMMITMENT AND FIDELITY

Vindicate me, O Lord, for I have walked in my integrity,
and I have trusted in the Lord without wavering.
I walk in my integrity; redeem me, and be gracious to me.
My foot stands on level ground; in the great congregation
I will bless the Lord.

PSALM 26:1, 11–12

PSALM 26 IS a poignant expression of the psalmist voicing his deepest needs before God. With humility, and yet with confidence, he asks for protection and guidance; he pleads with God to *examine* him and *try* his heart. When we respond to a passage of Scripture, a similar prayer may find its way into our hearts. Our response, *oratio*, is usually a spontaneous expression of a prayer that prays itself, or a poem that writes itself, or an image that forms itself.

BEHAVIORAL/MORAL SENSE

As we respond, *oratio*, to a passage of Scripture, we are ushered into what is called the behavioral/moral sense of Scripture. It is listening to Scripture to hear how Jesus calls us to live. It presupposes a level of faith and understanding that impacts how we hear and respond to Jesus' message in the Scriptures. When we experience the moral sense of Scripture, new insights begin to emerge, and we are drawn to live the Scripture message in the ordinary daily events of our lives. Keating writes:

> *As we repeat the phrase or sentence slowly, over and over, a deeper insight may arise. For example, take the words of Jesus, "I will not call you servants but friends." All of a sudden, it might come down on us what it means to be a friend of Christ. Our awareness expands without our having done anything but allow the Spirit to act. It is a heart-to-heart exchange with Christ. We think the text but we do not think about the text. If we are thinking in the sense of reflecting, we are dominating the conversation. That can be done fruitfully some other time. Here it is a question of receiving and resting in Christ's presence as the source of the word or phrase.[41]*

We experience the energy of Christ's light and truth within us, and we become light and truth.[42] Thelma Hall speaks of this dynamic in her book *Too Deep for Words*. She describes our desire for God as increasing when we begin to respond: "It is as though we are being drawn by a magnetic force in our own depths toward God as our center of gravity, where the center coincides with our true self."[43]

DRAWN INTO LOVE

A woman who experienced this magnetic force in her life's situation was Betsie ten Boom. Betsie and her sister Corrie, were imprisoned in a concentration camp during World War II. They had been caught hiding some of their Jewish neighbors in their home. Betsie was able to slip a copy of the Scriptures into the camp, and each evening she read the Scriptures and reflected with the women in their barracks. It gave them hope in a hopeless situation. Betsie not only shared the Scriptures with her cellmates; she responded to the Nazi guards with a kindness and compassion that could only be understood as an expression of the energy of Christ's light and truth within her. On her deathbed, with little of her own energy left, Betsie whispered to Corrie: "Corrie, we must tell people what we have learned here. We must tell them that there is no pit so deep that [God] is not deeper still. They will listen to us, Corrie, because we have been here."[44]

In the final moments before her death, Betsie used what little energy she had left to leave Corrie with a final message: "She moved her lips in reply but I [Corrie] could not follow. She formed the words again. I bent my ear to one side, level with hers. The blue lips opened again…'so much work to do…'"[45]

Even in her death, Betsie longed to give life to those who had taken her mortal life. The transformative power of the Word of God knows no limits if we are open and faithful.

A MOVEMENT OF THE HEART IN FAITH

Oratio, then, is a response, a movement of the heart, leading to *contemplatio*n. Our hearts are touched, and we are drawn to respond in love by living the Word of God. We let the Spirit guide us as we continue to listen and discern. Sometimes how we are to respond is not always clear and decisive. Rather, our ref*lectio*n on a passage of Scripture will bring us into ambiguity and confusion. At such times our *oratio* is but a request for guidance as we wait in patient receptivity. This is the nature of entering into relationship with the God of mystery. It is challenging because we are not usually comfortable with the unknown. We prefer knowing so we can respond decisively.

Mother Teresa knew this struggle of darkness well as she sought to respond to God's will. She shared her wisdom with a medical doctor who was suffering burnout and no longer found meaning and purpose in his profession. He had no idea how or where he wanted to spend the rest of his working years, but he knew he needed a change. He decided to take some time away to determine his future. Volunteering to help Mother Teresa's community by assisting in their care for the dying seemed like a good fit for him. After he arrived in India, he spent each day ministering in the Missionaries of Charity's hospital for the dying. One day, he was tending to one of the patients and Mother Teresa stopped by the hospital. She walked over to him and expressed her appreciation for his assistance in their ministry. In response he said to Mother: "Mother, please pray that God gives me clarity, so I will know what my future work will be."

Mother bluntly responded with a simple *"No!"* Taken aback by her response, he pondered her words until the next time he had the opportunity to speak with her. Then he asked her: "Mother, why did you refuse to pray that I be given clarity?"

Again she replied simply: "What we need to pray for is faith, not clarity!"

Mother Teresa's response underscores for us the truth that we are sustained by faith, not clarity. No matter how confused we may feel as we sort out our response to the call of the gospel, we can rely on our faith that God will guide us and slowly show us the way if we are willing to remain open and faithful. We can best express this openness and faithfulness by continuing to reflect on the Word of God as we listen attentively in the darkness.

There is need for discernment, even when the direction seems clear. A number of years ago a directee felt a strong call to *go to a different place*. The Scriptures she spent time with all seemed to affirm this message. She felt restless in her present ministry and desired more time for contemplative prayer. After much discernment she decided to spend a few months in a cloistered community. In time she discovered she had a terminal illness and needed to come home to die. Being in a *different place* became a significant part of where God was calling her, and it helped her prepare for her passing over from this life to the next. Her confusion was actually part of her journey. It was her faith that sustained her in all the uncertainty she was experiencing as she took various steps to respond; but she was always willing to adjust as her path unfolded.

DEEPENING AWARENESS

As we enter into dialogue with the Word—sharing our questions, fears, and apprehensions, taking small steps, testing out different possibilities—our *oratio*, our prayer, changes as we become more deeply aware of God's call at this time in our lives. Our *lectio divina* spills over into every dimension of our lives. We continue to ponder what is stirring within us, noticing what is happening in our daily lives. We notice in a reflective manner what other people say and do, and how we find ourselves responding or reacting. We begin to be aware of the attitudes and motivations behind our actions. This awareness gives us the freedom to choose how we might respond to a given situation.

As life unfolds, we often discover in hindsight what God is trying to teach us. This was very evident in a woman who was struggling with the death of her son. Shortly after losing her husband unexpectedly, Joyce received word that her youngest son, a college student, had been killed while hiking in the mountains near his school. He had been murdered by a sociopath by the name of Sam, who was later apprehended and sent to a prison psych ward. Joyce was overcome with grief, anger, and hatred. She could only rage at God and then beg for strength and guidance. She finally realized that she was being consumed by the rage she carried within, and she sought help from a number of support groups.

She finally was able to come to some acceptance and peace. However, she still found herself grappling with how she could learn from this tragic experience, and how God was asking her to respond. She continued to seek out retreats and other healing programs and eventually found herself at a Catholic retreat given for women. Although Joyce was a member of a Lutheran congregation, she felt very much at home participating in the daily eucharistic celebration. She believed in the eucharistic presence and desired to receive the sacrament. Her request to do so was granted by the retreat director. As she went toward the minister who was holding the cup, she was taken aback as the eucharistic minister turned away from her and returned the empty cup to the altar. Joyce did not know that the cup was empty. She interpreted the minister's action as a rejection of her very person. Heartbroken, she left the chapel and went to her room. She stretched out on her bed and cried herself to sleep. As she slept she dreamt that Jesus came to her and said: "Joyce, I have never refused you my cup, but no one has ever given my cup to Sam."

Joyce woke with a start, with the words of Jesus burned into her heart. After some reflection, she spoke with the retreat director and shared her story. He replied gently: "Have you forgiven Sam for murdering your son?"

Joyce responded that she believed she had. The retreat director then asked her: "Can you write to Sam and express your forgiveness?"

This request was more than Joyce could imagine, but she promised to pray about it. The director gave her the Prayer of St. Francis as a guide to her reflection:

Lord, make me an instrument of your peace.
Where there is hatred, let me sow love;
where there is injury, pardon;

where there is doubt, faith;
where there is despair, hope;
where there is darkness, light;
and where there is sadness, joy.

O Divine Master, grant that I may not so much seek
to be consoled as to console;
to be understood as to understand;
to be loved as to love.
For it is in giving that we receive;
it is in pardoning that we are pardoned;
and it is in dying that we are born to eternal life.
Amen.

After much prayer and *reflection*, Joyce felt called to write Sam a brief letter expressing her forgiveness. Relieved to have had the grace to write and send the letter, she found a new level of inner peace.

After a number of months, she received a letter from Sam thanking her for her letter and asking her to visit him. Again she found herself overwhelmed at the prospect, but in time she was drawn to make the trip to the prison and spend some time with Sam.

As she waited in the prison visiting area, she saw a young man coming toward her accompanied by a social worker. Sam was bent over as if he was carrying a heavy burden. As they began the visit, Joyce asked him to tell her what happened on the hiking trail and how he had killed her son. He shared with her that her son was just in the wrong place at the wrong time. He described her son's death and how his death had briefly relieved Sam's inner pain. Sam then began to talk about his life experience. On the streets from the time he was a young boy, he had never known a mother's love and had suffered endless abuse from the adults who crossed his path. Sam said he didn't believe in a God who could let such suffering and violence be inflicted on a child.

Joyce listened attentively and just let him share his story. When their time ended, Joyce wanted to reach out to him as a mother would to her wounded son, but she did not feel Sam would be able to receive her love. She said goodbye and promised to continue to write. In the following months, Joyce wrote many times to Sam and received his letters in reply. He continued to express his anger and question a God who would permit such suffering. Joyce never preached to Sam. Rather, she simply acknowledged his experience and then shared with him her experience of God. In time, Sam again asked Joyce to come for a visit. Once again she waited for him in the prison visiting area and soon saw a tall young man coming toward her with his social worker. There was a marked difference not only in his stature but in his eyes and in the expression on his face. His social worker said to Joyce: "He's getting well, and it is your letters that have brought him healing."

Sam spoke again of God and proclaimed that he still didn't believe in God but was beginning to consider ever so slightly the possibility of God's existence. As Joyce prepared to say goodbye, she again felt she wanted to give Sam a mother's hug, knowing that he had never been hugged by his own mother. She asked Sam: "Can I hug you?"

Sam initially looked at her in disbelief, and then he

replied, "Yes." Joyce hugged Sam, and as he turned to walk away he looked at his social worker and said: "She hugged me! She hugged me!"

As Joyce left the prison she remembered the words of Jesus in her dream: "I have never refused you my cup, Joyce, but no one has ever offered my cup to Sam."

Although Joyce's *lectio divina* was not the Scriptures as found in the books of the Bible, it was her prayerful reading of the Prayer of St. Francis, which was inspired by Francis's *lectio divina* on the words of Jesus. Her story gives us a sense of the power of *lectio divina*. She listened (*lectio*) with the ear of her heart, pondered (*meditatio*) what stirred within her, and responded (*oratio*) in a way she could have never anticipated. She became the presence of Christ in Sam's life. Her openness and receptivity to the movement of the Spirit within her allowed her to become the minister of Jesus' cup to Sam. Drawn into God's Spirit, she was transformed and became the *word* God created her to be.

GOD'S WORD STRETCHES US

The Word of God is constantly pulling us forward, stretching us, challenging us to greater awareness. We are called to continue to respond in faith as we live the questions and grapple with how we might respond in the most loving way. Jesus tells us in John's gospel, "If you continue in my word [*lectio divina*], you are truly my disciples; and you will know the truth and the truth will make you free" (John 8:31–32).

Our response in *lectio divina* can be a cry for help, a prayer for healing, a request for deepening faith, or a petition for an open and receptive heart. *Oratio* is our way of expressing what we need and desire in order to live the Word of God. It is a response that takes shape as we put ourselves at the disposal of the Spirit and let our heart be touched by the Word of God. Often the actual text drops out of consciousness. We move into a dialogue with God, asking our questions, expressing our struggle, and then responding to the One who has invited us to be in relationship. This behavioral/moral sense of Scripture is about the work of the Spirit in us; it is always characterized by freedom and by a new intuitive knowledge of God and the divine Word.

NURTURING OUR TRUE SELF

In time, our faithful practice of *lectio divina* slowly begins to transform our lives. As we listen and integrate into our lives the deeper meaning of God's Word, we find that it cuts through to our very essence, our true self, and nurtures the word we are meant to be. We may find ourselves being more open to forgive, less judgmental, more willing to reach out in compassion—as Joyce did. We begin to live the gospel message and take on the mind and heart of Jesus. Our falsity drops away, and we grow in receptivity to God's Spirit. Our human spirit becomes one with God's divine Spirit. Keating expresses the process succinctly in his book *The Heart of the World*:

> *Each period of lectio divina follows the same plan: reflection on the Word of God, followed by free expression of the spontaneous feelings that arise in our hearts. The whole gamut of human response to truth, beauty,*

goodness, and love is possible. As the heart reaches out in longing for God, it begins to penetrate the words of the sacred text. Mind and heart are united and rest in the presence of Christ. Lectio divina is a way of meditation that leads naturally to spontaneous prayer, and little by little, to moments of contemplation—insights into the Word of God and the deeper meaning and significance of the truths of faith. This activity enables us to be nourished by the "bread of life" (John 6:35) and indeed to become the Word of God (John 6:48–50).[46]

A SCHOLASTIC METHOD OF *LECTIO DIVINA*

PRELIMINARY COMMENTS:

The scholastic method of lectio divina *is a structured approach to this way of praying. There are four distinct steps, each one corresponding to a different aspect of the prayer. This method of* lectio divina *is helpful when teaching and when praying in a group setting. This exercise involves the first, second, and third moments of* lectio divina: lectio, meditatio, *and* oratio.

LECTIO: LISTENING TO THE WORD OF GOD OR READING GOD'S WORD

- Become quiet and consciously aware of God's presence. Pray for the gifts to listen with trust, humility, reverence, openness, and faith. Choose a passage from Scripture and read it as though for the first time.
- Listen to the Word of God as if for the first time; be aware of any word or phrase that catches your attention—a word or phrase.
- Begin to repeat that phrase, sentence, or one word over and over, allowing it to settle deeply in your heart. If any insights arise, do not expand these insights right now. This can be done at a later time. Simply return to the slow repetition of the phrase, sentence, or one word, savoring it in your heart.
- If so moved, share the word or phrase that caught your attention in the reading (applies to group setting).
- Allow a few moments of silence so that what you heard may sink deeper within.

MEDITATIO: PONDERING ITS MEANING

- Read the chosen passage from Scripture a second time. Notice what stirs within as you repeat the word or phrase that caught your attention. What is God saying?
- If so moved to do so, share what stirs within in response to the word or phrase that caught your attention (applies in group setting).
- Allow a few moments of silence so that what you heard may sink deeper within.

ORATIO: RESPONDING WITH COMMITMENT AND FIDELITY

- Read the passage for the third time. Now ask yourself: What is God's invitation?
- Write down your responses: a prayer, a poem, a desire you wish to fulfill.
- Formulate a prayer phrase that captures the essence of the passage for you.
- If so moved, share your prayer, poem, or other response to the message of the Scripture passage (group setting).
- Allow a few moments of silence to hold what you heard in reverence.

A MONASTIC METHOD OF *LECTIO DIVINA*

PRELIMINARY COMMENTS

The monastic way is unstructured—in a sense, methodless. One reads or listens to the Word of God in a particular passage chosen for the occasion, and then the only process is to follow the attraction of the Spirit.

THE MOMENT OF *LECTIO*

- Read the Scripture passage for the first time (it helps to read it aloud softly). What phrase, sentence, or even one word stands out to you? Begin to repeat that phrase, sentence, or one word over and over, allowing it to settle deeply in your heart. If any insights arise, do not expand these insights right now. This can be done at a later time. Simply return to the slow repetition of the phrase, sentence, or one word, savoring it in your heart.
- Relish these words; let them resound in your heart. Read the passage as often as you wish, learning these words by heart as you continue to repeat them in your mind.
- Let an attitude of quiet receptiveness—an openness to a deeper hearing of the Word of God—permeate your prayer time.

THE MOMENT OF *MEDITATIO*

- Let an attitude of quiet receptiveness permeate your prayer time. Be open to a deeper hearing of the Word of God.

- Sit with that phrase, sentence, insight, or word, repeating it gently over and over in your heart, not *thinking about it* but just being with it (pondering it in your heart).

THE MOMENT OF *ORATIO*

- Be aware of any prayer that rises up within you that expresses what you are experiencing (responding).

CHAPTER SIX

CONTEMPLATIO: **RESTING IN GOD WITH CONFIDENCE AND FAITH**

I wait for the Lord,
my soul waits.
And in his word I hope;
my soul waits for the Lord
more than those who watch for the morning,
more than those who watch for the morning.

O Israel, hope in the Lord!
For with the Lord there is steadfast love,
and with him is great power to redeem.

PSALM 130:5–7

THE EXPERIENCE OF waiting is not something that most of us relish. We tend to regard it with negative connotations and try to avoid such times or fill them with other tasks. Paradoxically, we find the psalmist in Psalm

130 waiting patiently with a positive outlook in hope and expectation. Waiting in this manner is a cherished time of preparation for the Lord with whom there is steadfast love and the power to redeem.

To wait in hope and expectation is the stance of a practitioner of *lectio divina* as she or he enters the fourth moment of the prayer. This moment of waiting is called *contemplatio*. St. Gregory the Great called it *resting in God*. It is a time of quiet and stillness. We wait with the Word, trusting and open to God's presence and call in our lives. We let it be done unto us as Mary, the Mother of God, did at the time of her annunciation. In a posture of receptivity, we give ourselves over to God's plan for us. Mary did not understand fully what was being asked of her. So too, we rest in God, letting ourselves be led into the unknown.

THE UNITIVE SENSE OF SCRIPTURE

The moment of *contemplatio* brings us to what the patristic fathers called the unitive sense of Scripture. This sense of Scripture leads us into an experience of oneness, of being where all opposites are reconciled. Conversation moves to communion, and we are assimilated to the Word and the Word to us. This sense corresponds to the level of union in a relationship and to the moment of *contemplatio*n, resting in the Word of God. We no longer experience a sense of separateness from God. Such oneness enables us to listen and respond to the gospel on ever-deepening levels of faith. The practice of *lectio divina* draws us more deeply into relationship with the Word of God. The Spirit within us enlightens us and takes us from what is most outward to what is most inward. The Spirit brings us into the abiding presence of God. "When we are in the unitive understanding of Scripture, the outward word confirms what we already know and experience."[47] When we are gifted with these moments of oneness, we are drawn into the Trinity. Participating in this mystery, "Christ-consciousness is so pervasive we pass through the low door of humility and take off hats and refrain from any speculation and bow in realization."[48]

A CONTEMPLATIVE MOMENT

During this time of resting with God we are invited to a place of interior quiet, tranquility, and peace with God, letting ourselves become silent and aware of God's presence. We willingly fall into the arms of God, resting in God's embrace, letting ourselves simply be with God. The Carthusian monk Guigo describes God's eagerness to be with us:

> *The Lord, whose eyes are upon the just and whose ears can catch not only the words, but the very meaning of their prayers, does not wait until the longing soul has said all its say, but breaks in upon the middle of its prayer, runs to meet it in all haste, sprinkled with sweet heavenly dew, anointed with the most precious perfumes, and [God] restores the weary soul...slakes its thirst...heeds its hunger...makes the soul forget all earthly things: by making it die to itself [God] gives it new life in a wonderful way...*[49]

The contemplative moment is a lingering with the insights and power of the conversation. It is also a proactive way to bring the fruit of *lectio divina* "which is experienced in the contemplative moment into daily life."[50]

Corrie ten Boom related such a moment in her book *The Hiding Place*. While Corrie and her sister Betsie were in the concentration camp, Betsie often spoke of the need to spread forgiveness after the war rather than to let anger and bitterness consume them. Betsie wanted to spend her post-camp days encouraging this spirit of forgiveness. But because Betsie died in the camp, Corrie resolved to fulfill Betsie's wish by bringing her message of forgiveness to all those touched by the Holocaust. One day Corrie was speaking to a church congregation in Munich. After her presentation she was greeting the members of the assembly as they left the gathering. Suddenly she saw him—the former S.S. man who had stood guard at the shower room door in the processing center at Ravensbruck. Suddenly, the insights of Betsie and her *lectio* on the need to forgive were blasted with a rush of memories that elicited anger and rage.

He came up to me...beaming and bowing. "How grateful I am for your message, Fraulein," he said. "To think that, as you say, He has washed my sins away." His hand was thrust out to shake mine. And I, who had preached so often...the need to forgive, kept my hand at my side.

Even as the angry, vengeful thoughts boiled through me, I saw the sin of them. Jesus Christ had died for this man; was I going to ask for more? "Lord Jesus," I prayed, *"forgive me and help me to forgive him."*

I tried to smile, I struggled to raise my hand. I could not. I felt nothing, not the slightest spark of warmth or charity. And so again I breathed a silent prayer. "Jesus, I cannot forgive him. Give him your forgiveness."

Then I was able to lift my hand; and as I took his hand the most increadible thing happened. From my shoulder along my arm and through my hand, a current seemed to pass from me to him, while into my heart sprang a love for this stranger that almost over-whelmed me.

And so I discovered that it is not on our forgiveness any more than on our goodness that the world's healing hinges, but on His. When He tells us to love our enemies, He gives, along with the command, the gift itself. [51]

A FOUR-STEP DANCE

As we rest, we may find ourselves being drawn back to one of the other moments of *lectio divina*. We may feel called to continue our dialogue with the Word, asking additional questions, pondering the deeper meaning of God's Word, and responding in faith. Or we may find ourselves rereading the passage we have chosen and experience ourselves being drawn to a different part of the reading. Hence, we may find that we want to reflect more deeply on what we hear being said to us (*meditatio*) or to continue the conversation (*oratio*) or to read the passage again (*lectio*). After this movement we may once again be drawn back into resting in the silence (*contemplatio*).

Whatever movement takes place, we trust the unfolding of our relationship with the Word. We follow its lead, letting ourselves be drawn more deeply into relationship with the deeper meaning of the Word. If we become distracted we can gently return to the initial word or phrase that caught our attention and repeat it quietly to ourselves. *Lectio divina* is like a four-step dance with God—reading, reflecting, responding, and resting with his Word. As we enter more fully into the inner rhythm of this dance, we experience an ever-deepening relationship with God's Word and Spirit. This prepares us to be open and receptive to the gift of experiencing God's presence—the gift of *contemplation*.

DEEPENING RELATIONSHIP

The story is told of a disciple who went to his master and said: "I want to be enlightened."

The master gave him several different ways of praying and disciplines to practice. After awhile, the disciple was discouraged, thinking that nothing was happening. He returned to the master and said: "I want something to happen because I'm getting tired of all these disciplines. What can I do to speed it up?"

The master said: "You cannot do anything to bring about your enlightenment any more than you can make the sun rise or set."

The disciple responded: "Then why am I doing all these exercises and practices?"

The master replied: "That's so you are awake when it happens."

The discipline of faithfully practicing *lectio divina* eventually awakens us. The scales drop from our eyes; not only do we become more attentive to God in daily life, but we grow in self-knowledge. We discover the source of the motivations and attitudes that shape our responses in daily life. We begin to sort out the wheat from the chaff and acknowledge both our gifts and limitations.

We also come to a fuller knowledge of who God is. False images of God give way to the truth found in the pages of Scripture. With God's Word as our guide, we come to know the mind and heart of Jesus Christ; and over time our spirit becomes one with God's Spirit.

The fruits of resting, of waiting, do not come easily. We often struggle to find time for a period of *lectio divina* in our lives. We get so caught up in the activities of our day that we find it difficult to listen, let alone be with another. Such a pattern of living leads to a feeling of being separate from God, which often results in a loss of faith in the God who loves us unconditionally and desires to be one with us. Even when we have the best of intentions, our spirit easily grows weary. Our daily activities continue to beckon us into the busyness that often consumes us. We become uncomfortable with resting in God's presence. It feels like a waste of our time. We are more comfortable being involved in an activity that we feel is meaningful and productive. We also find that the silence fills us with fear. We wonder: *What will happen if I rest in God's presence? What will I find within if I am silent? Maybe I have no depth. What will God ask of me?*

These fears keep us from letting go of our thoughts. Keating suggests that our thoughts are like boats in the harbor.[52] They prevent us from moving to a deeper level of awareness. In *lectio divina* we don't have to get rid of our thoughts but simply let them drift by and not engage in them unless they are relevant to the Scripture passage upon which we are reflecting.

The Desert Fathers and Mothers understood the difficulty we all have in letting go of our thoughts that lead us away from simply being in the stillness. They share with us the story of a novice who wanted to renounce the world.

A novice who wanted to renounce the world said to an old monk, "I wish to become a monk." The old man said, "You cannot." The novice said, "I can." The old man replied: "If you want, go, renounce the world, and sit in your cell." The novice went off and gave away what he had, withholding a hundred coins for himself, and came back to the old man. The old man said to him, "Go, sit in your cell." He went and sat down. While he was sitting, his thoughts said, "The door is old and wants replacing." The old man said to him, "You did not renounce the world. Go renounce the world and stay here." He went off, gave away ninety coins and hid ten coins for himself, and came back to the old man and said, "Look, I have renounced the world." The old man said to him, "Go, and sit in your cell." He went and sat. As he sat, his thoughts said to him, "The roof is old, and wants replacing." And going back to the old man, he said, "My thoughts are saying, 'The roof is old, and needs replacing.'" The old man replied, "Go, and renounce the world." He went

> *and gave away the ten coins, and came back to the old*
> *man and said, "Look, I have renounced the world."*
> *He sat down and his thoughts said to him, "Everything*
> *here is old, and a lion is coming to eat me up." He*
> *told the old man his thoughts, and the old man said to*
> *him, "I expect everything to come down upon me, and*
> *the lion to come and eat me up so that I may be set free.*
> *Go, sit in your cell and pray to God."[53]*

Not engaging in our thoughts during the time of resting in God's presence takes practice. We usually need to continually return to our sacred word, which, in *lectio divina*, is the word that caught our attention or a word that expresses the essence of the scriptural passage we are reading. This sacred word is a symbol of our intention to enter more deeply into the hidden meaning of the passage we have chosen and to consent to God's intention being expressed. The inner dynamic of our relationship with the Word is what determines the unfolding movement of our *lectio divina* experience. As we give ourselves over to this dynamic, we will be led into an ever-deepening relationship with the Word of God, which will change us and bring us into new life.

When we are resting quietly in God's presence, repeating as needed our sacred word, we need to let go of any expectations we might have of this quiet time. This time of prayer is usually not a time of great insights or awareness, but rather a time of our spirit *being with* God's Spirit in the quiet. We simply rest in God's presence, letting God's Spirit strengthen and transform us. This time of quiet rest, *contemplatio*, is comparable to moments of intimacy in a human relationship when there is no need for words.

Many years ago one of our sisters was taking care of her elderly parents. Her mother was quite confused, but her father was still very alert. I went to visit each month to support her in her care for her parents and her teaching ministry. One evening I was visiting with her in the kitchen as she prepared the evening meal. During a pause in our conversation she asked me to check on her mom and dad. I walked into the living room and found them sitting together on the sofa. Oscar was patting his wife, Lettia's, hand as she sat quietly next to him. As confused as Lettia was, she was able to rest and be at peace in his presence. I asked them: "What are you two doing?"

Oscar raised an eyebrow and with his customary sense of humor replied, "I'll never tell!"

I smiled. What was evident was that both of them were content to simply be with each other. There was no need to speak. Their presence to each other sustained them. This is what God wishes for us—to experience in faith God's presence with us and within us.

ONE WITH GOD

Spending time simply resting in God's presence is a prayer of faith that deepens our belief that we are one with God and that we are always in God's presence. As we become more aware of our oneness with God and all that God has created, we become a disciple of Jesus Christ in the fullest sense. We let ourselves be formed by his Word so we might radiate Christ's presence. As our relationship with God deepens, we desire not only to hear the Word but to become the word of God we were created to be. We wish to live as Jesus lived and respond as he responded and participate ever more fully in his life: "It is no longer I who live, but it is Christ who lives in me" (Galatians 2:20).

Lectio divina leads us on this path in a natural, organic way. It fosters a growing friendship with Jesus Christ that eventually brings an undifferentiated oneness of his Spirit and our spirit. This path is often a movement through darkness to light, from being asleep to being awake. It is a process of *catching* the moving light of God and finding him in diversity. A rabbinical story speaks of this movement:

> *An ancient rabbi once asked his pupils how they could tell when the night had ended and the day was on its way back. "Could it be," asked one student, "when you can see an animal in the distance and tell whether it is a sheep or a dog?" "No," answered the rabbi. "Could it be," asked another, "when you can look at a tree in the distance and tell whether it is a fig tree or a peach tree?" "No," said the rabbi. "Well, then what is it?" his pupils demanded. "It is when you look on the face of any woman or man and see that she or he is your sister or brother. Because if you cannot do this, then no matter what time it is, it is still night."*

In his article "The Classic Monastic Practice of *Lectio divina*," Keating describes the awakening to our oneness with all of creation that is the gift of *contemplatio*:

In contemplative prayer, we are in touch with the source of all creation; hence, we transcend ourselves and our limited worldviews. As a result, we feel at one with other people and enjoy a sense of belonging to the universe. The fullness of the Godhead dwells bodily in Jesus, according to Paul. The Divinity begins to dwell in us bodily in proportion to our capacity to receive it as we grow in union with the Eternal Word. This process needs to be nourished both by the interior silence of contemplative prayer and cultivated by lectio divina (in the sense of listening). The awareness of the divine presence will also begin to overflow into ordinary activity.[54]

In a letter to Sufi scholar Ch. Abdul Aziz, Thomas Merton describes his *contemplatio*: "It is not 'thinking about' anything, but a direct seeking of the face of the invisible, which cannot be found unless we become lost in him who is invisible."[55]

A SCHOLASTIC METHOD OF *LECTIO DIVINA*

PRELIMINARY COMMENTS

The scholastic method of lectio divina *is a structured approach to this way of praying. There are four distinct steps, each one corresponding to a different aspect of the prayer. This method of* lectio divina *is helpful when teaching and when praying in a group setting. This exercise involves the first, second, third, and fourth moments of* lectio divina: lectio, meditatio, oratio, *and* contemplatio.

LECTIO: LISTENING TO THE WORD OF GOD OR READING GOD'S WORD

- Become quiet and consciously aware of God's presence. Pray for the gifts to listen with trust, humility, reverence, openness, and faith. Choose a passage from Scripture and read it as though for the first time.
- Listen to the Word of God as if for the first time. Be aware of any word or phrase that catches your attention—a word or phrase.
- Begin to repeat that phrase, sentence, or one word over and over, allowing it to settle deeply in your heart. If any insights arise, do not expand these insights right now. This can be done at a later time. Simply return to the slow repetition of the phrase, sentence, or one word, savoring it in your heart.
- If so moved, share the word or phrase that caught your attention in the reading (applies to group setting).

- Allow a few moments of silence so that what you heard may sink deeper within.

MEDITATIO: PONDERING ITS MEANING

- Read the chosen passage from Scripture a second time. Notice what stirs within as you repeat the word or phrase that catches your attention. What is God saying?
- If moved to do so, share what stirs within in response to the word or phrase that caught your attention (applies in group setting).
- Allow a few moments of silence so that what you heard may sink deeper within.

ORATIO: RESPONDING WITH COMMITMENT AND FIDELITY

- Read the passage for the third time. Now ask yourself, "What is God's invitation?"
- Write down your responses: a prayer, a poem, a desire you wish to fulfill.
- Formulate a prayer phrase that captures the essence of the passage for you.
- If so moved, share your prayer, poem, or other response to the message of the Scripture passage (group setting).
- Allow a few moments of silence to hold in reverence what you heard.

CONTEMPLATIO: RESTING IN GOD WITH CONFIDENCE AND FAITH

- Read the passage for the fourth time.
- Rest with the passage, using as your sacred word the

word that captures the essence of the message.

- Continue to rest in God's presence, in God's embrace, using your sacred word to express your intention whenever your thoughts start drifting off.

- If you feel drawn back to the passage to read it again, ponder its meaning, or move into dialogue asking your questions, feel free to respond to the invitation to do so.

- Follow the movement of the Spirit within you as you find yourself in relationship with this word of God.

- Allow a few moments of silence to hold in reverence what you heard.

- End this prayer with the Our Father or another prayer that is fitting.

CLOSING PRAYER

Almighty God, thank you for the gift of your Word. May we take the word or phrase that spoke to us, the thought that we became aware of, and the prayer that came from our hearts, into the activity of our day (the time of retreat) as a reminder of our genuine desire to consent to your presence and action in our lives. We offer this prayer through Jesus Christ our Lord. Amen.

Gently ring the bell to end the session and leave, if appropriate, in silence.

A MONASTIC METHOD OF *LECTIO DIVINA*

PRELIMINARY COMMENTS

The monastic way is unstructured—in a sense, methodless. One reads or listens to the Word of God in a particular passage chosen for the occasion, and then the only process is to follow the attraction of the Spirit.

THE MOMENT OF *LECTIO*

- Read the Scripture passage for the first time (it helps to read it aloud softly). What phrase, sentence, or even one word stands out to you? Begin to repeat that phrase, sentence, or one word over and over, allowing it to settle deeply in your heart. If any insights arise, do not expand these insights right now. This can be done at a later time. Simply return to the slow repetition of the phrase, sentence, or one word, savoring it in your heart.

- Relish these words; let them resound in your heart. Read the passage as often as you wish, learning these words by heart as you continue to repeat them in your mind.

- Let an attitude of quiet receptiveness permeate your prayer time—an openness to a deeper hearing of the Word of God.

THE MOMENT OF *MEDITATIO*

- Let an attitude of quiet receptiveness permeate your prayer time. Be open to a deeper hearing of the Word of God.

- Sit with that phrase, sentence, insight, or word, repeating it gently over and over in your heart, not thinking about it but just being with it (pondering it in your heart).

THE MOMENT OF *ORATIO*

- Be aware of any prayer that rises up within you that expresses what you are experiencing (responding).

THE MOMENT OF *CONTEMPLATIO*

- Or just rest in the phrase, sentence, insight, or even one word—resting in God beyond your thoughts, reflections, and particular prayer, resting in God in the simple attraction of interior silence (resting).

CLOSING PRAYER:

Almighty God, thank you for the gift of resting in your Word. May we take the phrase, sentence, insight, or even one word that spoke to us and the prayer that came from our hearts into the activity of our day as a reminder of our genuine desire to consent to your presence and action in our lives. We pray that we may become this word through Jesus Christ our Lord. Amen.

Optional

After the closing prayer, ask the participants to join in a brief faith sharing that expresses in some way what they experienced with the Word of God. After the sharing, allow a few moments of silence so that what was heard may sink deeper within. Gently ring the bell to end the session.

CHAPTER SEVEN

BECOMING A WORD OF GOD

Blessed be the God and Father of our Lord Jesus Christ, who has blessed us in Christ with every spiritual blessing in the heavenly places, just as he chose us in Christ before the foundation of the world to be holy and blameless before him in love.

EPHESIANS 1:3–4

IN HIS LETTER to the Ephesians Paul reminds us that we are *chosen* by God "before the foundation of the world." It is difficult for us to wrap our minds around this mystery of being always in the mind of God and being chosen by him. Robert Mulholland, in his book *Shaped by the Word*, helps us unpack the full import of these words. He traces the meaning of the word *chose* and notes that it comes from the Greek words *ek*, out of, and *lektos*, to speak. Thus we might define chose as to be spoken forth.[56] With this understanding we can read the passage from Ephesians as: *God spoke us forth...before the foundation of the world.* As such we can each identify ourselves as a *word* of God spoken forth *to be holy and blameless*. Acknowledging who we are—*a word of God* spoken in love—helps us understand our most basic and essential vocational call to become fully who we were created to be.

Thomas Merton also saw our call as an invitation to become a *word* of God. He speaks of our creation as a process that happens from within, with God's grace. Our meaning and purpose reflects God's truth and "makes me his 'word' spoken freely in my personal situation."[57] Our true identity can be found in God's "call to my freedom and my response to him."[58]

Such a call reveals not only who we are meant to be but also who God is. As a word of God we each give expression to a unique aspect of God. Just as many words make up a sentence and many sentences create paragraphs, so in a faith community we come together as many unique *words* of God, and together we become God's presence to each other. There is no need to compare ourselves to others. We cannot say that we are a better word than someone else. Sometimes the smallest *word* manages to hold the whole paragraph together. We need to honor the word God made each of us to be. God's deepest desire for us, our holiness, is to become fully who he created us to be with our particular gifts and limitations.

SHAPED BY THE WORD OF GOD

A very natural, organic way to become who we are meant to be is to deepen our relationship with the Word of God through the practice of *lectio divina*. The dynamic that is initiated by faithfully reading, reflecting, responding, and resting with the Scriptures is one that leads us to listen with the ear of our heart to the ground of our being and hear God's creative Word resonating within us and drawing forth who we are called to be. It is a transforming moment as we come to know ourselves as one of God's words who is to mirror God's Word as expressed in the Scriptures. It is an experience "which, at one and the same time, reveals God's life in us and our life in God."[59]

As we are faithful to the practice of *lectio divina*, we discover that the very core of our being, our true self, is a word of God called to bring God's presence into consciousness. The call is for us to live out of the ground of our being where God's Spirit and our spirit are one. This means letting go of our idealized self, our distorted ego, and allowing God's Spirit to slowly reshape and purify our perceptions, perspectives, and attitudes in accord with the mind and heart of Jesus Christ.

Lectio divina helps us come to know the Scriptures and give us insights into the ways in which God's Word penetrates human lives and situations. It reveals the truth of the human condition, addresses our brokenness, and calls us into wholeness. It transforms the flawed words we have become into the words God wants to speak forth to be in the world.[60]

As we encounter the living, penetrating Word of God, we are invited into a whole new way of being with God.[61] It is a process that does not happen unless we are willing to be open and receptive to entering into dialogue with God's Word and surrendering in trust and faith. Such vulnerability is only possible when we know we are loved by God, who is bringing us into wholeness and forming us into fullness of life.

The process of becoming a word of God unfolds much like a human relationship between a disciple and a master. Initially, the disciple feels a call to enter into relationship with the master and makes every effort to follow the master's directives. As the disciple grows in familiarity and trust of the master, he or she begins to hear with the ear of the heart the deeper meaning of the master's directives and is given the grace to respond wholeheartedly. This response in turn strengthens the commitment and bond of the disciple with the master, and intimacy deepens. In time the disciple desires only to be one with the master, to have the disciple's spirit united with the master's spirit.

Coming to such oneness is also the intent of the practice of *lectio divina*. We begin by listening (*lectio*) attentively to the Word of God as found in the Old and New Testament. This initial step of listening (*lectio*) soon gives way to reflecting (*meditatio*) on how the meaning of the Word of God touches our lives. This ref*lectio*n (*meditatio*) brings us face to face not only with our hopes but also with our fears, which often present themselves as questions, dilemmas, and apparent contradictions. At this point we either choose to take the next step and delve deeper into the mystery of who God is and who we are called to be as a word of God, or we decide to walk away. This is the moment of hearing the call and responding (*oratio*).

MOVEMENT TO GOD

Such a response was forthcoming from Ralph, a young man who was tortured with thoughts of suicide. Ralph's father had taken his own life, as had Ralph's brother. Deeply grieved by the loss of their presence in his life, Ralph feared he would make the same choice. These were the thoughts that occupied his mind as he walked past a neighborhood church each day. Finally, he decided to spend some time in the church; he slipped into the back bench and just sat in the quiet. He found this quiet time comforting, so he regularly took time to sit in the silence for a brief period. Eventually, Ralph realized that he felt safe in the church. He had a sense that he was in God's presence, and he did not have thoughts of suicide. He wondered how he could take God's presence with him wherever he was, so he would always feel safe. He decided to speak with the priest at the church rectory. Knocking on the rectory door, he asked to see the priest and then shared with him his question: "Can you teach me how to be in God's presence?"

The priest encouraged him to spend time each day reflecting on a passage of Scripture. He gave him some passages and encouraged Ralph to come back in a week. When Ralph returned he shared with the priest his experience and the insights that had come to him as he reflected on the Scripture passages. The priest listened, encouraging him and gently affirming the inner stirrings that Ralph shared. After a number of weeks, Ralph began to notice that he no longer was bothered with thoughts of suicide. Instead, he found himself repeating certain words or phrases of the Scriptures that lingered with him. He experienced himself in the presence of God's Word. He felt safe wherever the activities of his day took him. Ralph's decision to move *toward* God's Word rather than *away* made all the difference in whom he was becoming—a person with meaning and purpose.

If we continue to grapple with how the message of God's Word speaks to our lives, as did Ralph, we will often be brought to our knees in deep gratitude and an inner freedom and peace that sustains us in the midst of life's struggles. As Jessica Powers expresses so beautifully in her poem *The Mercy of God*, we are brought from fear to freedom:

I am copying down in a book from my heart's archives
the day that I ceased to fear God with a shadowy fear.
Would you name it the day I measured my column of
virtue and sighted through windows of merit a crown
that was near?
Ah, no, it was rather the day I began to see truly that
I came forth from nothing and ever toward nothing-
ness tend,
that the works of my hands are foolishness
wrought in the presence of the worthiest king in a
kingdom that never shall end.
I rose up from the acres of self that I tended with pas-
sion and defended with flurries of pride;
I walked out of myself and went into the woods of
God's mercy,
and here I abide.
There is greenness and calmness and coolness, a soft
leafy covering
from the judgment of sun overhead, and the hush of
His peace, and the moss of His mercy to tread.
I have naught but my will seeking God; even love
burning in me is a fragment of infinite loving and
never my own.

*And I fear God no more; I go forward to wander forever
in a wilderness made of His infinite mercy alone.*[62]

In the penetrating truth of Jessica Powers' poetry, we find
expressed our journey—a movement from self to God. She
describes it as a growing awareness of our nothingness, a
stepping out of self and into the experience of God's infinite
mercy. This path leads us into the mystery of God's unconditional love and leaves us with a deep sense of gratitude for
God's mercy and compassion. Humbled before such love,
we find deepening within us a desire to become fully, with
God's grace, the word we are created to be.

This path challenges us to live in a manner congruent
with Jesus' life and to trust that, if we continue to be attentive to the Word of God, we will be shown the way. We
no longer simply go through the Scriptures, but we let the
Scriptures go through us.

It is at this time in our relationship that a commitment
of friendship is made. Open and receptive to the move-
ments of God's Spirit in our lives, we respond by letting
God's Word shape us and mold us as God so designs. This
commitment leads us, the disciple, into a full participation
in the life of God.

COURAGE TO CONSENT

Thus, the regular practice of *lectio divina* has the power to
transform us if we give ourselves over day after day. God
dismantles our falsity and we are free to step out of our small
ego-centered mind and into the mind and heart of Jesus

Christ. With Paul we can say: "I live now, not I, but Christ lives in me" (Galatians 2:20).

This oneness is further deepened and solidified as we rest (*contemplatio*) and consent in the presence of the Word, repeating the one Word of God that is a symbol of all that God is drawing forth FROM within us. Slowly our falsity is dismantled, and we are no longer bound by the many self-centered demands of our ego. What gives purpose and meaning to our lives begins to change. It is no longer about being successful, being affirmed, being secure or in control. Rather, we recognize that our deepest call is to be a unique word of God, a messenger of God's presence—who is with us, loving us into fuller life. We can let God's Spirit be center stage in our lives.

Corrie and Betsie ten Boom, of *The Hiding Place,* became God's presence for the many women and men in the camp with them. Betsie often told Corrie: "If these people can be taught to hate, they can be taught to love! We must find the way, you and I, no matter how long it takes…"[63] The words of Scripture were written on their hearts, and they responded accordingly. Like Betsie and Corrie, we begin to see as God sees, and we come to know that "nothing is more beautiful than the uniqueness that God has created"[64] in each human being.

FROM FEAR TO INNER FREEDOM

It is a journey from fear to inner freedom. As we bring to the events of daily life an awareness of being in the presence of God, every event is experienced as a revelation of God. We find ourselves more attentive and able to listen with the ear of our heart to how God is speaking in each moment and in all of creation. All is in God, and God is in all. With such oneness, our energy becomes one with divine energy. With Christ, the energy of God's mercy, we become more merciful. With the Father, the energy of God's compassion, we become more compassionate. With the Spirit, the energy of the love relationship between Father and Son, we become more loving. Filled with God's energy we become fully the word God created us to be: *"holy and blameless before God"* (Ephesians 1:4).

A WAY OF LIFE

Just as *lectio divina* is a way of praying that deepens our relationship with God, so too in time it becomes a way we live. We discover God's presence hidden in all the events of our daily lives. We are attentive to the events of daily life, reflecting on them, pondering, letting them speak to us. We may notice that our perspective begins to shift. Often the shift is most apparent in our changing image of God. We recognize that our image of God today is not the image of God we had as a child. Cardinal Basil Hume describes this transformation in his experience of reaching for a cookie in his mother's cookie jar. When he was a child, he thought God was going to slap his hand if he took a cookie between meals. As an adult, his image of God had changed. Now he knew God's unconditional love, and each time he reached for a cookie he heard God say, "Take two!"

We also begin to notice changes in ourselves as the fruits

of *lectio divina* find fertile ground within us. We discover more of who God is as we step out of our self-made image of ourselves and hear for the first time God's words:

I am with you.
I love you.
Trust me!

We know well our weaknesses and vulnerabilities, but we have also experienced God's love embracing us as we are. Our lives become a witness of this love in gratitude for God's patience with us and God's merciful forgiveness.

Our practice of *lectio divina* provides a way to respond to God, who is pursuing us and loving us into the fullness of life. God receives our faithfulness by honoring us with a call to a deepening relationship and bringing us into oneness with all of creation. If we are willing to stoop low enough to listen, to embrace our humanity in all humility, to accept reality as it is, and to admit our needs, then God will bring us into fullness of life and we will become the word God created us to be.

We have God's promise reflected in Scripture, in the early church fathers, and in contemporary expressions of poetry. In Scripture, we hear the words of Ezekiel: "I will give you a new heart, and place a new spirit within you, taking from your bodies your stony hearts and giving you natural hearts" (Ezekiel 36:26).

In an effort to express the wisdom of the early church fathers and mothers, John Cassian describes the transformation of our hearts as we become a word of God praying without ceasing:

That perfect love of God, by which "he loved us first,"
will have also passed into our heart's disposition…
and then every love, every desire, every effort, every
undertaking, every thought of ours, everything that we
live, that we speak, that we breathe, will be God…
whatever we understand…will be God.[65]

Finally, our transformation process is described poetically through an adaption of the message of Caryll Houselander's modern spiritual classic *The Reed of God*. Houselander compares us to a reed that needs to be hollowed out so that we can be an instrument of God's music. As the Divine Therapist heals our inner wounds and cleans out the inner junk that blocks us, we are called to be God's instrument. When we surrender, we receive the gift of understanding, and a whole new world opens for us. It is the Word of God that guides us in this new land of promise. It is a process of becoming a *reed of God* as expressed by Sister Rosemary Dauby in her poetic rendition of Houselander's book:

We are emptiness like the hollow in the reed,
the narrow rift less emptiness which can have only one
destiny: receive the piper's breath and to utter the song
that is in the piper's heart.

We are emptiness like the hollow in the cup, shaped to
receive water.

We are emptiness like that of a bird's nest.
The reed grows by the streams.

It is the simplest of things, but it must be cut by the sharp knife, hollowed out, stops put in it.

It must be shaped and pierced before it can utter the shepherd's song. It is the narrowest emptiness in the world, but the little reed utters God's infinite music.

We are lifted up and carved out, formed and shaped and filled with all the music of the earth.[66]

CHAPTER EIGHT

LECTIO ON LIFE:
DWELLING IN POSSIBILITIES

Hear a just cause, O Lord; attend to my cry; give ear to my prayer from lips free of deceit. From you let my vindication come; let your eyes see the right. I call upon you, for you will answer me, O God; incline your ear to me, hear my words. Wondrously show your steadfast love, O savior of those who seek refuge from their adversaries at your right hand.

PSALM 17:1–2, 6–7

AS A WAY of listening to the Scriptures and fostering our relationship with Jesus Christ, *lectio divina* can also be a means of letting the events, relationships, and situations of our life speak of how God is present and active in our lives. At times it is fitting to simply sit down and read the experiences of the last few days or weeks, much as we might slowly read and savor the words of Scripture in *lectio divina*. This is called *lectio on life*, and it gives us a means to uncover God's gentle presence in the midst of our lives. The meaning and purpose of our lives is often hidden by the confusion of the moment and the limited understanding we have of any situation. With the psalmist we often cry: "Hear a just cause… attend to my cry…" (Psalm 17:1).

Lectio on life provides us an opportunity to revisit such events and discover God's presence in the midst of what initially appears as confusing or challenging. I remember arriving home shortly after my father died of a heart attack. His presence was very evident in everything around the house—such objects as his favorite chair, his old trousers hanging in the garage, and his golf clubs all spoke of his deafening absence. In time, as I revisited the days following his sudden death, I saw that what had been signs of his absence became signs of both his presence and God's presence in the midst of a deep sense of loss. Such a shift in perspective is possible if we are open to hear how God is present in daily life. It often takes us some distance from a troubling event to revisit and hear how God is present—trying to teach us, to free us of our insecurities, and to help us embrace the truth. As Keating says: "Difficulties give God the opportunity to refine and purify our motivation. They give us an opportunity to make a greater surrender."[67]

MINDFULNESS

If we are to become who God created us to be, we need to be attentive and receptive, letting ourselves be formed and shaped by the sacred Scriptures as well as by the scriptures of our lives. What this really calls for—and what is so difficult for us—is to live in the present moment. We tend to be either considering the future, or we move into the past and spend a lot of time with regret, trying to rearrange reality. Rather, we need to accept what is and ask: *God, how are you present here?*

How differently our days might unfold if we brought to them a keen awareness of God's presence in the midst of the ordinary. What would it be like if we sat down for dinner fully present to each person and attentive to the stirrings within oneself? What would we notice? What would catch our attention? What would we tend to ignore? How would we respond or not respond as the conversation unfolded? Would we notice the texture of the food and savor the taste rather than eating in a functional manner?

I remember one of our sisters during her retreat making a decided effort to open both her physical and spiritual senses. She later recounted that as she ate breakfast she noticed, as if for the first time, the uniqueness of the grapefruit before her. She looked at the grapefruit, and her attention was drawn to the divisions that made up its whole. Then she noticed all the little pods of juice, the symmetry of each section, and how each part integrally made up the whole. In this contemplative moment the beauty of the grapefruit overwhelmed her, and she was moved to tears of gratitude and joy for the gift of God's creation.

Being contemplative is about being aware and awake to God's presence in the ordinary. It is not about having esoteric experiences or being privy to prophetic messages. It's about taking a *long, loving look* at all that is. Becoming women and men of *lectio* teaches us to ponder the mystery of God's presence and action in our lives, to see all that is through the eyes of a loving God. It is to be open to possibilities, as Emily Dickinson said it so well in one of her poems:

> *I Dwell in Possibility,*
> *A fairer house than Prose,*
> *More numerous of windows,*
> *Superior of doors.*
>
> *Of chambers, as the cedars –*
> *Impregnable of eye;*
> *And for an everlasting roof*
> *The gables of the sky.*
>
> *O visitors – the fairest –*
> *For occupation – this –*
> *The spreading wide my narrow hands*
> *To gather Paradise.*[68]

INFORMATION OVERLOAD

But it is difficult to be attentive when we are bombarded by information. The documentary *What the Bleep Do We Know?* claims that scientists have found as many as 4,000 bits of information coming into our awareness at any given time, and that we are only able to grasp about 200 of them. We want to be in the know, to know what's going on, and yet we miss most of the information available to us. This tension causes us to block out anything we are not able to take in, and we end up seeing only what we want to see rather than being open to all the possibilities in the present moment that are there for us to explore.

If we take time to do *lectio on life*, we begin to open ourselves to God's presence in the ordinary and in all of creation. Sometimes it's not too difficult to find God in the beauty of creation, but the challenge is to find God in the person who gets under our skin or irritates us. To accept another just as they are and to love them unconditionally is the call of being a disciple of Christ. The story of our lives is our sacred scriptures that need to be read with the ear of our heart.

ACTIVE PRAYER PHRASE

The practice of *lectio divina* often gives us an active prayer phrase to take into our daily activities and enrich our *lectio on life*. It can open us to new insights, new awareness, and the hidden meaning of an event. We may find a shift in our awareness or a change in our perspective. One morning, I began my time of prayer with a short reading from Michael Casey's book *The Road to Eternal Life*. In his book Casey reflects on the Prologue of the Rule of St. Benedict, line by line. On this morning I opened the book to line 10 of the Prologue, a quote from Psalm 95: "Today, if you hear (God's) voice, harden not your hearts."

Casey speaks at length of the source of our hardness of heart. He identifies four causes: "forgetfulness of God, the pursuit of trifles, defective self-knowledge, and, finally, its counterpart, defective self-acceptance."[69]

I tucked this information away and began my *lectio divina* by reading a passage from the Acts of the Apostles that encourages the disciples to speak the Word of God with boldness: "Grant to your servants to speak your word with all boldness, while you stretch out your hand to heal, and signs and wonders are performed through the name of your holy servant Jesus" (Acts 4:29–30).

As I reflected on "speaking the Word with boldness," I found myself contrasting this stance with the "hardness of heart" of which Benedict speaks. Obviously the two are diametrically opposed to each other. The contrast continued to play itself out as the day unfolded. Listening to a directee describe her anger with someone who was upsetting her daily routine brought the hardness of heart to the forefront again as we explored her deeper need for a security that was not being met. She recognized her tendency to hold too tightly to the symbols of security she had identified in her life and how this hardness of heart was blocking her relationship with God and others. Later in the day I found myself wrestling with a decision about taking on additional ministry. I was challenged by one of my sisters and found myself resisting her suggestion that it would not be wise to add to an already full schedule. Finally, I was able to identify my own hardness of heart in my refusal to listen to the advice of another. Thus the Word of God that caught my attention in the morning continued to inform me throughout the day and to grace me with new insights and a greater openness.

This is how the fruits of our prayer come in the midst of daily life. Often others notice the change in us before we do ourselves. One man who faithfully practiced resting in the silence asked his wife if she noticed any change in him. Her response was: "I don't know what you are doing, but please continue. You are much easier to live with."

We may also find that we are able to listen to others and respond rather than react. The discipline of letting go of our thoughts in prayer helps create a healthy relationship between ourselves and our thoughts. We find that we more readily listen to the different nuances of what a person is saying and are able to respond to the essence of their message. We discover in our daily life an underlying rhythm of God reaching out to us through Jesus Christ and our response of offering ourselves.

Lectio on life, then, helps us establish a gentle rhythm in our lives between times of ref*lectio*n and times of activity.[70] If one is daily growing in the art of finding Christ in the pages of the Bible, one naturally begins to discover him more clearly in aspects of the other things he has made. This includes, of course, our own personal history. Very often our concerns, our relationships, and our hopes and aspirations naturally intertwine with our pondering of the Scriptures, as has been described above. As we sit down and are attentive to the scriptures of our lives as they are being written, we can attend with the ear of our hearts to our own memories, listening for God's gentle presence in the events and happenings of the ordinary. We thus allow ourselves the joy of experiencing Christ reaching out to us through our memories—and our personal story becomes our history.

LECTIO ON LIFE[71]

Applying lectio divina *to my personal salvation history*

Purpose: to apply a method of prayerful reflection to a life/work incident (instead of to a Scripture passage)

Listening for the Gentle Touch of Christ the Word

(Lectio—Reading)

- Quiet your body and mind: relax; sit comfortably but alert; close your eyes; be attuned to your breathing...
- Gently review events, situations, sights, encounters that have happened during the last week or month in your life.
- Focus on one event or relationship that draws your attention, being attentive to what you notice.

Gently Ruminating, Reflecting *(Meditatio—Meditation)*

- Continue to focus on your life experience.
- Recollect the setting, sensory details, sequence of events.
- Notice where the greatest energy seemed to be evoked. Was there a turning point or shift?
- In what ways did God seem to be present? To what extent were you aware then? Now?

Prayerful Consecration, Blessing *(Oratio—Prayer)*

- Use a word or phrase from the Scriptures to inwardly consecrate—to offer up to God in prayer—the incident and interior ref*lectio*ns.
- Allow God to accept and bless your response and continue to lead you on the way.

Accepting Christ's Embrace; Silent Presence to the Lord

(Contemplatio—Contemplation)

- Remain in silence for some time.
- After a period of silence, you may wish to journal about your *lectio* on life.

LECTIO ON LIFE WORKSHEET

THE TRANSFORMING POWER OF *LECTIO DIVINA*

LISTENING FOR THE GENTLE TOUCH OF CHRIST THE WORD
(LECTIO—READING)

- Quiet your body and mind: relax; sit comfortably but alert; close your eyes; be attuned to your breathing...
- Gently review events, situations, sights, encounters that have happened during the last week or month in your life.
- Focus on one event or relationship that draws your attention, being attentive to what you notice.
- If you wish, write what stirs within you.

_____

_____

_____

_____

_____

_____

_____

_____

GENTLY RUMINATING, REFLECTING *(MEDITATIO—MEDITATION)*

- Continue to focus on the life experience.
- Recollect the setting, sensory details, sequence of events.
- Notice where the greatest energy seemed to be evoked. Was there a turning point or shift?
- In what ways did God seem to be present? To what extent were you aware then? Now?
- Enter into conversation or dialogue with God about your event/relationship/situation.

_____

_____

_____

_____

_____

_____

_____

PRAYERFUL CONSECRATION, BLESSING (*ORATIO—PRAYER*)

As you continue to reflect on how God was present speaking in the event, respond in your own words to God through a prayer, a poem, or any expression that writes itself and captures what is in your heart. Allow God to accept and bless your response and continue to lead you on the way.

_____

_____

_____

_____

_____

_____

_____

_____

ACCEPTING CHRIST'S EMBRACE; REST IN THE SILENT
PRESENCE OF GOD (*CONTEMPLATIO—CONTEMPLATION*)

- Choose a word or phrase that captures the essence of this experience or symbolizes a new insight or meaning that you have discovered.
- Simply rest with the experience, repeating the word silently to yourself.
- You may find yourself drawn back into the memory. Follow the lead of your inner stirrings.

_____

_____

_____

_____

_____

_____

_____

_____

STEPPING-STONE EXERCISE

Sometimes we can facilitate our *lectio on life* by engaging in a stepping-stone exercise that opens for us all the periods of our lives. Our stepping-stones represent periods or chapters in our lives around which a lot of events have happened. We read the scriptures of our lives in a *lectio* manner and try to be attentive to what God is saying to us.

Close Your Eyes and Focus on the Present Moment

- Let yourself become still within. (Pause)
- Focus on your breath, breathing in and breathing out.
- As you breathe in, be open to a deeper awareness of God; and as you breathe out, pray for a deeper awareness of all the ways that God reveals God's self to you.

Review Your Life History

- Focus on your life story, your personal history of salvation, how God has been with you through the years.
- Sit in the silence, and let the events, the relationships, the situations that have shaped you into who you are today come to you; jot them down.
- They may not come in chronological order, but you can order them later.
- Jot down whatever comes to mind as you think back over your life, the events, the situations, the relationships—whatever it has been that has shaped you into who you are today.
- Write ten or twelve stepping-stones as you rest in the silence. They don't have to be something spiritual; they can be as common as an old shoe.
- Put the list in chronological order.
- Read them back to yourself so you get a feel of the movement of your life.

Read, *Lectio*

- Choose a stepping-stone period in your life that was confusing or about which you have lingering questions. Choose one of the stepping-stones and describe this time in two or three paragraphs.
- Read to yourself the description you have written. Listen to it as though you hear it for the first time.
- Be attentive to what you notice. There may be something that happened within that situation that comes to mind again.
- Take note of where your energy is.

Reflect, *Meditatio*

- As you ponder this time in your life, be attentive to what stirs within you.
- How has this period of time affected your life?
- Did God seem present or absent during this time?
- Was there or is there an invitation or a call?

Respond, *Oratio*

- What response surfaces within you?
- If a prayer surfaces, let it find space within you to pray itself.

Rest, *Contemplatio*

- Spend just a few moments resting in the experience, consenting to God's presence and action during this time of your life.
- In faith, consent to whatever God is trying to teach you.
- If you find yourself going back to this time, pondering it some more, follow the lead of the Spirit whether you feel drawn to listen (*lectio*), to reflect (*meditation*), to respond (*oratio*), or to continue to rest (*contemplation*).

CHAPTER NINE

LECTIO DIVINA AND CENTERING PRAYER

*[God] spread a cloud to cover them and fire to give them light
by night. They asked, and [God] brought them quail, and
with bread from heaven he satisfied them. [God] cleft the rock,
and the water gushed forth, it flowed through the dry lands
like a stream, for [God] remembered his holy word to his servant Abraham. And [God] led forth his people with joy, with
shouts of joy [God's] chosen ones.*

PSALM 105:39–43

OUR JOURNEY THROUGH the desert of life is filled
with many challenges and sufferings as well as joys and blessings. Yet in the midst of these blessings and trials, God, in a
gentle way, is with us and brings us through life's experiences
in a way that deepens our relationship with God and brings

us into fullness of life. Sometimes our way of being with God is to listen intently to God's Word and then to reflect, respond, and rest with God's Word as we hear it addressed to us. This is the way of praying that is called *lectio divina* or divine reading of the Scriptures, which we have considered in the chapters of this book. At other times we find ourselves drawn into the silence, and we simply desire to rest in God's embrace, consenting to God's presence and action in our lives. This is a way of praying that is called centering prayer. Although there is interplay between these two ways of prayer, there is also a distinction.

The first distinction between *lectio divina* and centering prayer is that *lectio divina* is participatory. This means that we use all our faculties—our imagination, our intellect, and our will—just as we would in any relationship. We actively engage in relationship with the Word, listening, reflecting, responding, and resting with the Word of Scripture that speaks to us. As we dialogue with the Word in *lectio divina*, we ponder its meaning and then respond to its invitation. We are actively engaged in our relationship with the Word, receiving insights and new awareness, and responding to the promptings of the Spirit. On the other hand, centering prayer is more receptive. We simply open ourselves to receive God's presence and consent to God's intention for our lives. Our stance is one of receptivity as we rest in God's presence. We come with an openness and receptivity before God that is a complete surrender.

Because *lectio divina* involves a more active participation, it is necessarily a concentrative way of praying. We read and reflect on the Word of God so we might hear its meaning and then respond to, and rest with, its message. We concentrate our attention on the meaning of the Word as we might concentrate the rays of the sun with a lens. Centering prayer, on the other hand, is more receptive. We come open, ready to surrender to God's intention for our life—to be the glory of God fully alive.

> *It is not you that shape God*
> *it is God that shapes you.*
>
> *If you are the work of God*
> *await the hand of the artist*
> *who does all things in due season.*
>
> *Offer him your heart,*
> *soft and tractable,*
> *and keep the form*
> *in which the artist has fashioned you.*
>
> *Let your clay be moist,*
> *lest you grow hard*
> *and lose the imprint of his fingers.*[72]

The content of *lectio divina* and centering prayer is also distinctive. The preferred content for *lectio divina* is sacred Scripture. Whether we read a parable from the synoptic gospels or choose a few verses from a passage of Scripture, our content is the Word of God. In centering prayer there is no content other than our sacred word, which is a symbol of our intention to consent to God's presence and action in our lives. We are open to go beyond thought because of *being attracted by the mysterious and absorbing presence of the Spirit.*[73]

Lectio divina stresses our relationship with God through

the use of thoughts, images, and insights. This is the natural, organic way that *lectio divina* deepens our personal relationship with God. We learn who God is and who we are and how our relationship brings us into fullness of life. Centering prayer also nourishes our relationship with God, but by focusing on the moment of intimacy inherent in any relationship. Hence, we are encouraged to let go of thoughts, images, and insights in an effort to enter into the silence of God's transforming presence. This act of surrender opens us to God's presence and action within us and frees us to be messengers for Christ (2 Corinthians 5:20).

Probably what is most distinct in these two ways of praying is the moment of rest. In *lectio divina* the time of rest is not sustained. It comes and goes; it is not permanent. Having dialogued with the Word of God, we may find ourselves drawn to the quiet to simply be with the meaning of the Word as it has come to us. Our sacred Word at this time becomes the word or phrase that caught our attention as we reflected upon the Scripture. We rest and let the Word deepen within us until we feel drawn back into the dialogue. Another question may arise or a new clarity may come to us. We continue to communicate with the Word until we once again are drawn back into the silence.

In centering prayer the time of rest is sustained for at least twenty minutes. We are able to continue our period of rest in centering prayer by the use of a sacred word. As a symbol of our intent to consent to God's presence and action in our lives, we gently repeat the sacred word whenever we find ourselves becoming engaged in our thoughts. This is with the intent to nourish our time of intimacy with God.

INTERPLAY BETWEEN *LECTIO DIVINA* AND CENTERING PRAYER

If these two forms of prayer are used together, it is helpful to have a period of centering before a time of *lectio divina*. Centering prayer clears our minds, helps us step away from our thoughts, and prepares us to listen to the Word. In this sense, centering prayer is a gift to *lectio divina*.

> *It diminishes three obstacles to the journey: over con-ceptualization, hyperactivity and over dependence on self. Centering Prayer helps us get beyond these obstacles and settle into the quiet as we listen to the scriptures,* Lectio Divina, *in a contemplative manner. Centering Prayer opens us to new thoughts, new action and a deeper dependence on God.*[74]

Lectio divina as a prayer form also supports our practice of centering prayer. It deepens our personal relationship with God and draws us to rest in God's transforming presence.[75]

The interplay between centering prayer and *lectio divina* was evident in the experience of Sister Ildephonse, one of my sisters who found that her times of quiet drew her to a prayerful reflection on Psalm 139. After spending a day in quiet dialogue with the psalm, she was graced with a deep-ening awareness of God's love for her. In amazement and gratitude she captured the experience by saying: "I never would have known how much God loves me if I hadn't taken this retreat day."[76] She never would have known if she hadn't followed her intuition to spend a day in prayer with an old, familiar psalm. She read it one more time as if for the first time, and God's transforming presence overwhelmed her. Resting in the quiet led to a rich experience of *lectio divina*, which in turn gave way to a moment of intimacy. Her faithfulness prevented her from falling into the temptation of being blocked by the familiarity of the text. Instead, she heeded the wisdom of Dom Bernardo Olivera: "The wise person knows that it is one thing to know the chemical formula of water and another to savor it by a spring on a summer's day."[77]

In a poem by Father Harry Hagan, O.S.B., we hear expressed a similar bit of wisdom:

> *Read—*
> *and feed a little while upon the words*
> *that you may heed their heart and then be spurred*
> *to pray and plead with Christ, the only Word,*
> *until both you and we be freed and stirred*
> *for him, the seed who grows within unheard*[78]

APPENDIX

The integrity of the practice of lectio divina *is retained by being faithful to a few simple guiding principles.*

- Begin with a prayer to the Holy Spirit.

- The Spirit is the divine source of *lectio divina*.

- Be open to the divine presence within self.

- The Spirit is the guide to all truth.

- Be spontaneous and creative.

- Start at any of four moments, wherever one feels called.

- Read Christ into the Old Testament as the fathers and mothers of the church did.

- Read the New Testament as if one is reading about one's own experience of grace.

- Memorize and put on the Scriptures in mind and heart.

- Be open on all levels of one's being.

- Listen as God speaks to the different levels of one's being, i.e., imagination, memory, will, reasoning, reflective and intuitive faculties.

- Be faithful when the Spirit moves toward intuitive faculties and prayer becomes dry.

- Trust that God is calling one to a deeper union, relationship, and communion.

- Read the gospel stories as parables of grace.

- Read your experience of grace into the gospels and see them as parables of grace.

- Let the external word awaken the interior Word.

- Be aware of one's limitations.

- Know that one's interpretation of Scripture is limited.

- Acknowledge that one's interpretation is determined by where one is coming from.

- Receive one's insights as for today; receive others tomorrow.

- Move from more to less:
    - From reading a lot to reading less.
    - From reflecting a lot to reflecting less.
    - From praying a lot to praying less; from saying prayers to being in prayer.
    - Resting a lot, even in the midst of activity.

SELECTED BIBLIOGRAPHY

Arico, Carl. *Taste of Silence*. New York: Continuum Publishing Co., 1999.

Arntq, William, Chasse, Betsy, and Vicente, Mark. Directors. DVD: *What the Bleep Do We Know?* California: Captured Light Industries, 2005.

Attridge, Harold W. *The HarperCollins Study Bible*, New Revised Standard Version. San Francisco: Harper San Francisco, 2006.

Barnhart, Bruno, OSB Cam. *Monastic Forum*, St. Meinrad, IN, January 11–12,1998.

Benedict, XVI. Reflections on Dei Verbum, Address, Rome, Italy: Castel Gandolfo, September 16, 2005.

Bianchi, Martha and Hampson, Alfred, eds. *Poems by Emily Dickinson*. Boston: Little, Brown and Co., 1942.

Bruun, Mette. *Parables: Bernard of Clairvaux's Mapping of Spiritual Topography*. Leiden, Netherlands: Koninklijke Brill NV, 2007.

Casey, Michael. *The Road to Eternal Life*. Collegeville, MN: Liturgical Press, 2011.

Cassian, John. *The Conferences*. New York: Newman Press, 1997.

Catechism of the Catholic Church. Washington: United States Catholic Conference, Inc., 1994, 2008.

Cummings, Charles, OCSO. *Monastic Practices*. Kalamazoo, MI: Cistercian Publications, 1986.

Dauby, Rosemary. *Reeds of God*. Unpublished poem. Ferdinand, IN: Sisters of St. Benedict, 2005.

Dorff, Francis. *The Journey from Misery to Ministry*. Notre Dame, IN: Ave Maria Press, 1998.

_____, Francis. *The Art of Passing Over: An Invitation to Living Creatively*. New York: Paulist Press, 1988.

Dysinger, Luke, OSB. *Accepting the Embrace of God: The Ancient Art of Lectio Divina.* Valyermo, CA: Valyermo Benedictine Saint Andrew's Abbey, Spring, 1990 (vol.1, no.1).

Fry, Timothy, ed. *Rule of Benedict.* Collegeville, MN: The Liturgical Press, 1982.

Funk, Mary Margaret. *Lectio Matters.* New York: Continuum Publishing Co., 2010.

Griffiths, Paul. *Religious Reading: The Place of Reading in the Practice of Religion.* New York: Oxford University Press, 1999.

Guigo. *The Ladder of the Monks.* Translated by Edmund Colledge, OSA, and James Walsh, SJ. Kalamazoo, MI: Cistercian Publications, 1981.

Guigo. *The Ladder of Four Rungs.* Edited by James Hogg. Scala Claustralium. Cambridge, MA: Cambridge University Library, 2003.

Hall, Thelma. *Too Deep for Words.* Mahwah, NJ: Paulist Press, 1988.

Kardong, Terrence, OSB. *Together Unto Life Everlasting: An Introduction to the Rule of Benedict.* Richardton, ND: Assumption Abbey Press, 1984.

Keating, Thomas. *Awakenings.* New York: The Crossroads Publishing Company, 1990.

_____, Thomas. *The Better Part.* New York: Continuum, 2000.

_____, Thomas. *The Classic Monastic Practice of Lectio Divina.* Article, Butler, NJ: Contemplative Outreach, 2000.

_____, Thomas. *Foundations for Centering Prayer and the Christian Contemplative Life: The Mystery of Christ.* New York: The Continuum International Publishing Group, Inc., 2002.

_____, Thomas. *The Heart of the World.* New York: Crossroads Publishing Co., 2008.

_____, Thomas. *Heartfulness: Transformation in Christ Workbook.* Wilkes-Barre, PA: Contemplative Outreach Media Center, 2009.

_____, Thomas. *Intimacy with God.* New York: Crossroads, 1994.

Laird, Martin. *Into the Silent Land.* New York: Oxford University

Press, 2006.

Leclercq, Jean. "*Lectio divina*," Worship 58 (1984).

Merton, Thomas. *Contemplative Prayer*. New York: Random House, 1996.

_____, Thomas. *The Seven Storey Mountain*. San Diego, CA: Harcourt Brace, 1948.

Mulholland, Robert. *Shaped by the Word*. Nashville, TN: Upper Room Books, 2000.

Nowell, Sr. Irene, OSB. *The Bible Today: The Word of God*. Collegeville, MN: The Liturgical Press, January/February 2012.

Olivera, Dom Bernardo, OCSO. Sentences on '*Lectio divina*,' Liturgy (OCSO) 26.3, 1992.

Potter, Mike, ed. *Lectio Divina Presenters Handbook*. Butler, NJ: Contemplative Outreach Ltd., 2012 Edition.

Potter, Mike, Maria Tasto, Leslee Terpay, and George Welch. *Lectio Divina* Service Team. *Lectio Divina* Immersion Retreat Conferences. Butler, NJ: Contemplative Outreach, Ltd., 2011.

Powers, Jessica. *The Selected Poetry of Jessica Powers*. Washington, DC: ICS (Institute of Carmelite Studies) Publications, 2000. All copyrights, Carmelite Monastery, Pewaukee, WI.

Robertson, Duncan. *Lectio Divina: The Medieval Experience of Reading*. Collegeville, MN: Liturgical Press, 2011.

Senior, Donald. *Give Us This Day*. Collegeville, MN: Liturgical Press, Vol. VIII, December 2011.

Stewart, Columba. *The World of the Desert Fathers*. Oxford, England: Fairacres Publication 95, 1986.

Studzinski, Raymond. *Reading to Live*. Collegeville, MN: Liturgical Press, 2009.

Ten Boom, Corrie. *The Hiding Place*. Grand Rapids, MI: Chosen Books, 2008.

ENDNOTES

1.   Benedict XVI. *Reflections on Dei Verbum* (address delivered in the courtyard of the papal summer residence of Castel Gandolfo. September 16, 2005).

2.   Ibid., 1.

3.   Jean Leclercq, "*Lectio Divina*," Worship 58 (1984), 239.

4.   Ibid., 247.

5.   Sr. Irene Nowell, OSB, *The Bible Today: The Word of God*. (Collegeville, MN: The Liturgical Press, January/February 2012), 21.

6.   Timothy Fry, Ed., *The Rule of Benedict in English* (Collegeville, MN: The Liturgical Press, 1982), 15.

7.   Donald Senior, *Give Us this Day* (Collegeville, MN: Liturgical Press, December 2011, Vol. VIII), 324.

8.   Mette Bruum, *Parables: Bernard of Clairvaux's Mapping of Spiritual Topography* (Leiden, Netherlands: Koninklijke Brill NV, 2007), 119.

9.   Raymond Studzinski, *Reading to Live* (Collegeville, MN: Liturgical Press, 2009), 22. Statement summarizes Paul Griffiths book *Religious Reading: The Place of Reading in the Practice of Religion* (New York: Oxford University Press, 1999), 41.

10. Ibid., 25.

11. Thomas Keating, *Awakenings* (New York: The Crossroads Publishing Company, 1990), ix–x.

12. Over the centuries the application of the senses of Scripture to the different moments of *lectio divina* has been somewhat ambiguous. The area of confusion has been with the second (*meditatio*) and third (*oratio*) moments. Scholars, however, generally agree that *meditatio* reflects the allegorical sense of Scripture and *oratio* the behavioral/moral sense. Their

thought is that the movement of the prayer is from words/ concepts to wordless/response. Father Thomas Keating in his writings takes the less familiar path of aligning the behavioral/ moral sense with *meditatio* and the allegorical sense with *oratio*. His approach flows from both a relational and psychological understanding of how a friendship develops and leads to intimacy. Father Thomas Keating understands the behavioral/moral sense of Scripture as one's response to a call. It is a way of responding to the expectations inherent in the call. Thus, after hearing the literal sense of Scripture we reflect and ponder the call and its subsequent expectations for us. Following this schema, Father Thomas Keating identifies the third moment of *lectio divina*, *oratio*, with the allegorical sense of Scripture. He understands the allegorical sense as leading to a deeper understanding of the Scripture message. We explore the meaning of the passage for us and we enter into conversation and dialogue with Christ as we move toward a response. In the natural flow of any relationship the different moments are interchangeable and have no set order. Thus, *lectio divina* as a prayer that nourishes our relationship with God is methodless. All of the moments together enrich each other and bring to fullness the call to intimacy.

13. Keating, *Awakenings*, x–xi.

14. Studzinski, *Reading to Live*, 20–139.

15. Guigo, *The Ladder of Four Rungs,* James Hogg, ed. (Scala Claustralium. Cambridge, MA: Cambridge University Library, 2003), 253–327.

16. Duncan Robertson, *Lectio Divina, the Medieval Experience of Reading* (Collegeville, MN: Liturgical Press, 2011), 230.

17. Ibid., 173.

18. Robert Mulholland, *Shaped by the Word* (Nashville, TN: Upper Room Books, 2000), 51.

19. Ibid., 52.

20. Fry, *Rule of Benedict*, 15.

21. Thomas Keating, *Foundations for Centering Prayer and the Christian Contemplative Life: The Mystery of Christ* (New York: The Continuum International Publishing Group, Inc., 2002), 295.

22. William Arntz, Betsy Chasse, and Mark Vicente, directors, DVD: *What the Bleep Do We Know?* (California: Captured Light Industries, 2005).

23. Thomas Keating, *Intimacy with God* (New York: Crossroads, 1994), 126.

24. Cancer Patient, Caring Bridges, 2012. http://2Cor129km. wordpress.com/.

25. Retreatant, *A Transformed Life* (Encino, CA: Holy Spirit Retreat House, September 2004).

26. Curé of Ars. Reference unknown.

27. Mike Potter, Maria Tasto, Leslee Terpay, and George Welch, *Lectio Divina* Service Team. *Lectio Divina* Immersion Retreat Conferences (Butler, NJ: Contemplative Outreach, Ltd. 2011), 8.

28. Martin Laird, *Into the Silent Land* (New York: Oxford University Press, 2006), 3.

29. Thomas Keating, *The Better Part* (New York: Continuum, 2000), 40.

30. Matisse, Henri. Reference unknown.

31. Keating, *Intimacy with God*, 46 ff.

32. Francis Dorff, *The Art of Passing Over: An Invitation to Living Creatively* (New York: Paulist Press, 1988), 11.

33. Fry, *Rule of Benedict*.

34. Potter, et al., *Lectio Divina*, 8.

35. Note in the *HarperCollins Study Bible* (2006) on Ps 34:7.

36. *Catechism of the Catholic Church* (Washington, DC: United States Catholic Conference, Inc., 1994, 2008), 650.

37. Mary Margaret Funk, *Lectio Matters* (New York: Continuum

Publishing Company, 2010), 31.

38. Potter, *Lectio Divina*, 12.

39. Ibid., 11.

40. Keating, *The Better Part*, 41–42.

41. Thomas Keating, "The Classic Monastic Practice of *Lectio Divina*" article (Butler, NJ: Contemplative Outreach, 2000).

42. Potter, *Lectio Divina*, 14.

43. Thelma Hall, *Too Deep for Words* (Mahwah, NJ: Paulist Press, 1988), 43.

44. Corrie ten Boom, *The Hiding Place* (Grand Rapids, MI: Chosen Books, 2008), 227.

45. Ibid., 228.

46. Thomas Keating, *The Heart of the World* (New York: The Crossroads Publishing Co. 2008), 48.

47. Keating, *Intimacy with God*, 53.

48. Funk, *Lectio Matters,* 141.

49. Guigo, *The Ladder of the Monks*, trans. Edmund Colledge, OSA, and James Walsh, SJ (Kalamazoo, MI: Cistercian Publications, 1981).

50. Potter, *Lectio Divina*, 17.

51. Ten Boom, *The Hiding Place*, 247–248.

52. Keating, *Intimacy with God*, p. 62

53. Columba Stewart, *The World of the Desert Fathers* (Oxford, England: Fairacres Publication 95, 1986), 2.

54. Keating, "The Classic Monastic Practice of *Lectio Divina*."

55. Thomas Merton, *The Seven Storey Mountain* (San Diego, CA: Harcourt Brace, 1948), 433.

56. Mulholland, *Shaped by the Word*, 34.

57. Thomas Merton, *Contemplative Prayer* (New York: Random

House, 1996), 68.

58. Ibid.

59. Francis Dorff, *The Journey from Misery to Ministry* (Notre Dame, IN: Ave Maria Press, 1998), 169.

60. Potter, *Lectio Divina*, 20.

61. Ibid.

62. Powers, Jessica, *The Selected Poetry of Jessica Powers*, Washington, DC: ICS (Institute of Carmelite Studies [ICS] Publications, 2000), 1. All copyrights, Carmelite Monastery, Pewaukee, WI. Used with permission.

63. Ten Boom, *The Hiding Place*, 175.

64. Thomas Keating, *Heartfulness: Transformation in Christ Workbook* (Wilkes-Barre: Contemplative Outreach Media Center, 2009), 1.

65. John Cassian, *The Conferences,* 10: VII, 1–2 (New York: Newman Press, 1997), 375–376.

66. Rosemary Dauby, *Reeds of God,* unpublished poem (Ferdinand, IN: Sisters of St. Benedict, 2005).

67. Keating, *Foundations for Centering Prayer,* 272.

68. Martha Bianchi and Alfred Hampson, eds. *Poems by Emily Dickinson* (Boston: Little, Brown and Co., 1942), 289.

69. Michael Casey, *The Road to Eternal Life* (Collegeville, MN: Liturgical Press, 2011), 37.

70. Luke Dysinger, *Accepting the Embrace of God: The Ancient Art of Lectio Divina (*Valyermo, CA: Valyermo Benedictine Saint Andrew's Abbey, Spring, 1990), vol.1, no.1.

71. Ibid. This is a free interpretation of *Lectio* on Life as outlined by Fr. Luke Dysinger.

72. Attributed to Saint Irenaeus.

73. Keating, *Intimacy with God*, 146.

74. Potter, ed., *Revised LD Handbook,* Handout #2.

75. Ibid.

76. Sr. Ildephonse Retzer, OSB, conversation with author, date unknown.

77. Dom Bernardo Olivera, OCSO, "Sentences on '*Lectio divina*,'" Liturgy (OCSO) 26.3 (1992); 89.

78. Fr. Harry Hagan, OSB, personal communication with author, date unknown.

79. Potter, Mike, ed. *Lectio Divina Presenters Handbook* (Butler, NJ: Contemplative Outreach Ltd., 2012 edition), 38.